Finding the Living

John E. Hunter

OF THE ZONDERVAN CORPORATION
GRAND RAPIDS, MICHIGAN 49506

FINDING THE LIVING CHRIST IN THE PSALMS

Grand Rapids, Michigan

Sixth printing 1976

Library of Congress Catalog Card Number 70-189587

Appreciation is expressed to the following publishers
for permission to quote from their translations of the Bible:

THE MACMILLAN COMPANY for their permission to use verses
from *The New Testament in Modern English.*
Copyright © 1958, 1959, 1960 by J. B. Phillips.

ZONDERVAN PUBLISHING HOUSE for permission to quote from
The Amplified Bible. Copyright © 1965 by the
Zondervan Publishing House. *The Amplified New Testament.*
Copyright © 1958 by The Lockman Foundation.

Printed in the United States of America

Contents

1

Finding the Key

The Book of Psalms has always had great significance in the Christian Church. It is used in daily services, and provides the means of worship in the Episcopal Church. The Messianic Psalms play a great part in our study of the Christology of the Old Testament.

But I want to use this book, *Finding the Living Christ in the Psalms,* to share with you something that has been a great blessing to my soul. Some of these thoughts have already been shared with others, and they have encouraged me to write them in a book so that I can develop the ideas and put them in a permanent form.

First, let me give you a key. Keys are wonderful things, not for what they are, but because of where they can lead you. I found such a key some time ago. I have used it to open many doors. When I went through each door my heart was blessed. This Key will open one hundred and fifty doors. But let me show you how I found it.

Luke 24 is the great chapter on the resurrection. It opens into a new world and introduces us to a most blessed Person—the risen Christ. We meet our blessed Lord as He joined the two on the walk to Emmaus. We know how sad they were, confused and upset. Then the risen Christ spoke to them these time-echoed words:

O fools, and slow of heart to believe all that the prophets have spoken.

Ought not Christ to have suffered these things, and to enter into his glory?

And beginning at Moses and all the prophets, he expounded unto them in all the scriptures the things concerning himself (Luke 24:25-27).

What a glorious Bible study that must have been. It covered the whole of the Old Testament. Notice how it says "beginning at Moses." Those are the five books of Moses, called the Pentateuch. Then it says "all the prophets"—major and minor. It is wise to pay special attention to the word "all" whenever you meet it in the Bible. I draw a circle around each one I see. They are vital. When the Bible says "all" it means "all." "All the prophets . . . all the scriptures," is a wonderful phrase. It means that the Lord gave His imprimatur to the whole of the Old Testament. He underwrote it, He established it, He vindicated "all the scriptures"—and that term includes all our Old Testament.

In verse 44 He is with His own in the upper room. His first appearance produced fear, which soon changed to joy. Then He said these remarkable words:

These are the words which I spake unto you, while I was yet with you, that all things must be fulfilled, which were written in the law of Moses, and in the prophets, and in the psalms, concerning me.

Then opened he their understanding, that they might understand the scriptures (verses 44, 45).

Again our Lord is referring to the Scriptures, but in a new and exciting way. He said: "all things must be fulfilled . . . concerning me." Now notice who the "me" is—this is the risen, victorious Christ speaking in all His risen power. He said there are many things to be fulfilled, but notice which special books He referred to. This is where my own soul was really blessed. I saw, in a new way, the tremendous significance of the Psalms.

The Lord Jesus specifically referred to the Psalms. He said you will find "me" in the Psalms. There are new things to find, new blessings to experience, new treasures to discover, new promises to claim—all in the Psalms.

This then was my key. I was going to find Jesus in the Psalms. I had a Key that would open one hundred and fifty doors—each door being a Psalm. I have not been into all of them yet. Only a few have been my special joy, so far. But let me take you with me as we put the key in the lock, and push gently, and find Jesus in the Psalms.

Always remember that whenever you find the living Christ you find reality. That is what makes this journey so worthwhile—to find a Savior who is real, living and who has so much more for us today.

It is possible to study the Bible in truth and with sincerity, but in such a way that the main result is only an increase in academic knowledge. The area of belief is enlarged, but the capacity to turn that belief into behavior remains as ineffective as ever before. A belief without a corresponding behavior is a sterile thing. There is a lack of warm joy and radiant peace. The witness given, if any, is only an academic statement of belief, not a ringing testimony to reality.

It is my prayer that as we look into these Psalms we may find the living Christ, that He may find us, and that this mutual discovery will bring to our hearts a new quality of daily living. In John 14:19 the Lord Jesus said: "Yet a little while, and the world seeth me no more: but ye see me: because I live, ye shall live also." There is the promise—"but ye see me: because I live, ye shall live also."

May we see Him—the living, risen, victorious Christ — and because He lives, may we start to live also, here and now in this broken, troubled world.

2

The Mystery of the Two Hands

Psalm 23

In this treasury we call "The Book of Psalms," there are many that stand out with special significance. Some of the Psalms contain isolated precious truths that instill courage into failing hearts. But, surely, the best known, the best loved in the whole gallery of grace is Psalm 23, the Shepherd Psalm.

Hymn writers have delighted in taking the jewels of truth and arranging them into an ornament of beauty. There are more hymns based on this Psalm than on any other. It comes as an extra challenge to consider that David wrote these words over 3,000 years ago. Just consider any other words written so many years ago. If we could read them, how dusty and irrelevant they would seem — like dry bones poking through the ashes of history.

See the fresh, crisp relevance of these words of David. Notice that all the pronouns are singular, personal pronouns. It could have read: "The Lord is our shepherd; we shall not want." That would have been true in every sense, but the truth would have lost its cutting edge. The penetrating blessing of this Psalm is the personal touch — "*my* shepherd" — "he maketh *me*"—"he leadeth *me*"—"thou art with *me*." There is something unique in sensing the individual attention of the shepherd for each one of His sheep. Counting through the Psalm in the King James version we find that the words "I," "my," and "me" occur seventeen times, "He" and "His" thirteen times. So in these six short verses we have the personal relationship emphasized thirty times. What a precious thought.

Not only is it personal, bringing the words right to the heart, but it also speaks of the present. This is one of the thrilling aspects of this Psalm. For 3,000 years these words have been alive, day by day. It could have read: "The Lord was my shepherd," or "The Lord will be my shepherd," and, in each case, this would have been true. But the value of this Psalm is to feel it living and breathing, as a vital relevant experience. Speaking of the Lord in Psalm 121 we read: "Behold, he that keepeth Israel shall neither slumber nor sleep" (verse 4). How true this is of the Shepherd Psalm—it neither slumbers nor sleeps. Just as we read in Luke 2:8 of the shepherds abiding in the field, keeping watch over their flock by night, so the fragrance of this Psalm can penetrate into the lonely, long hours of a night of waiting and watching. Its voice can come as a whisper to the tired soul, infiltrating into the inner recesses of a crushed spirit. Each day as we wake and go forth to the tasks ahead of us we can lay hold of each phrase as a tower of strength—"The Lord is my shepherd; I shall not want."

I have found great comfort in reading the Psalm verse by verse then, after each verse, to bring in as a chorus the words, "all the days of my life." Try it and see how it underlines the personal, present tense experience: "The Lord is my shepherd; I shall not want—all the days of my life."

But, apart from these thoughts, the real deep well-spring of blessing will never be ours unless we look at the other side of the Shepherd Psalm. Psalm 23 gives us only one aspect of the Shepherd relationship. It shows us the picture from the point of view of one of the flock. This is the sheep speaking, telling of the Shepherd relationship in day-by-day experience. If we turn to John 10 we can hear the Shepherd speaking. Jesus said we would find Him, the risen Christ, in the Psalms. It is a joy to make this discovery concerning the One who is the Good Shepherd.

In verse 11 we read: "I am the good shepherd: the good shepherd giveth his life for the sheep," and in verse 14 He says: "I am the good shepherd, and know my sheep, and am known of mine."

But let us turn to verses 27-30 and discover the other side of the Shepherd Psalm:

> *My sheep hear my voice, and I know them, and they follow me:*
>
> *And I give unto them eternal life; and they shall never perish, neither shall any man pluck them out of my hand.*
>
> *My Father, which gave them me, is greater than all; and no man is able to pluck them out of my Father's hand.*
>
> *I and my Father are one.*

Here we have the Shepherd speaking about His sheep, just as in Psalm 23 the "sheep" was telling of the Shepherd.

See the same personal thrust in these verses: "My sheep . . . my voice."

There are three important ideas we can learn as we go on to study the verses. First, they tell us of "The Greatest Security" in all the world of human experience.

Coupled with our search is the study of the mystery of the two hands. This is what these verses are all about—two hands.

Speaking of His sheep the Lord says in verse 28: "I give unto them eternal life . . . neither shall any man pluck them out of my hand." Most speakers use their hands to help them communicate their words. This is true in ordinary conversation, and more true with certain people, but especially is it so with a preacher. In John 10 the Lord is preaching and teaching the mystery of the two hands, so surely He will use His two hands to illustrate His point.

He shows how secure the believer is by putting "him" into His "hand." There he is safe in the hand of Christ —no one can pluck him out. The King James Version says: "Neither shall any man pluck them out of my hand." The word "man" is in italics, which means that the word was not in the original but was inserted by the translators to make sense—in their estimation.

So what the Lord really says is that His sheep have eternal life, they will never perish and no one — no man, nor demon, nor devil — can ever pluck them out of His hand. He put them there, each one, and they are safe for all eternity.

Then in verse 29 He goes on to speak about His Father's hand. He says His Father is greater than all and no man—or demon—or devil is able to pluck them out of His Father's hand. As Jesus speaks these words He goes through the motions of putting the believer in the other hand—His Father's hand.

As the people watch and listen they follow the teaching of His lips and the movements of His hands. They see the believer placed into security in one hand—the hand representing the hand of Jesus. Then they see the believer placed into security in the other hand — the hand representing the Father. They watch and wonder —how can I be in two hands at once?

There is a way whereby you can be in two hands at once—only one way. And that is what Jesus teaches in verse 30. Can you see Him moving His hands as He speaks these words: "I and my Father are one"? He brings "the Father's hand" and cups it over His own hand, so that both hands are together, one above the other.

As the people look they see the perfect illustration of "greatest security." They imagine a precious soul cupped in the hand of Christ, covered by the hand of

"hollow of his hand"

the Father. No one can ever pluck them out of the place of maximum security.

This is what the people see as they watch the moving, teaching hands of Jesus.

Now what Jesus said to them is true for us also. If we have trusted Him as our Savior, then we are one of His sheep. Then we, too, are cupped and covered in the two blessed hands—and no one can ever pluck us out—Jesus said so!

This knowledge of being safe in the two hands has some beautiful consequences, if only we follow through with the idea.

I counsel with Christians whose lives are full of fear and worry and anxiety. They see themselves in all their weakness facing up to a hard, cruel world, but, notice where they are afraid, notice where the fear and anxiety grip their souls — it is in the two blessed hands that keep and hold. Surely this should make a difference in our attitude—there we are, safe in the hands where no man can rob or hurt—Jesus said so!

There are others who are lonely. I am finding that one of the biggest sources of pain and sorrow in the world is loneliness. I think of parents whose children have grown up and left them; husbands and wives whose loved one has left them—either by death or divorce; young people who are lonely in a world full of people. Yes, loneliness has a crushing, deadening effect, but, notice, where we are lonely—in the hands of Jesus—He said so!

He said: "I will never leave thee nor forsake thee" (Heb. 13:5), and He meant it. And this is how He can do it, by putting us in His hands — He said so. Surely this should bring to us a sense of nearness, if only we will believe what He said. This then is the teaching on "maximum security," and it can be ours through the risen victorious Christ—the One who said, "You will find Me in the Psalms."

Then, secondly, this same Psalm can teach us "Maximum Success." There are Christians who know the

Psalm, believe the Psalm, love the Psalm and yet the experiences it describes never come their way. They have no experience of lying down in green pastures, of being led, of having their soul restored, of having a prepared table in the midst of enemies. Their cup does not run over—in fact, in some cases it is empty and dry. There must be a reason for this.

If you really want to know "maximum success," then first you must be able to say, "The Lord is my shepherd." Then you must be able to really mean it when you say, "And the Shepherd is my Lord." Every true believer knows Jesus as his Savior. He has been to the cross, confessed his sin and received Christ as the Savior who died for him. This he does gladly, then he rejoices in being saved. But, if this is all he does then he is facing a Christian life fraught with failure and disappointment. The key to success is knowing the Shepherd as your Lord.

The angel who announced the birth of Christ as recorded in Luke 2:10, 11 said: "Fear not: for, behold, I bring you good tidings of great joy, which shall be to all people." Notice that his message was planned to bring great joy to all people, yet many Christians do not have great joy. In fact, there are many who have no joy at all—only distress and failure. See now what was the message that was designed to bring this great joy: "For unto you is born this day in the city of David a Saviour, which is Christ the Lord." It was not only Christ the Savior, but "a Saviour which is Christ the Lord."

Verse 14 tells us the outcome of such a relationship with the Savior and Lord: "Glory to God in the highest, and on earth peace, good will toward men." Three things come when Jesus is Savior and Lord. First, our lives bring glory to God; second, we have peace in our hearts; and last, there is a radiant outflow from our lives that touches and warms the hearts of those around us.

See how impoverished is the life of the Christian who

knows the Shepherd only as Savior. I see them everywhere, in all countries, of all ages—no joy, no glory, no peace, no good will!

The Lordship of Christ in the life of the believer is the absolute essential priority in daily living. Then, why do so many Christians content themselves with knowing Him only as Savior? There are several reasons—one is ignorance. They have never been taught the relationship of the believer with the risen Christ. Knowing only the half truth they have received, they have no capacity to go on to a full relationship.

Another reason for recognizing Jesus only as Savior is simply this—it costs too much to go any further. To know Him as my Savior costs me nothing. Salvation is the free gift of God. Jesus paid it all. All I do it take what God gives, and the blessing is mine. But to call Him Lord, and to mean it, makes a totally different relationship.

This refers to the time when there were lords and slaves. The lord owned the slave, who then became his property. The slave had no rights at all, he had no possessions—all that he was belonged to his lord. It is this same relationship that has to exist between the believer and Christ the Lord. First Corinthians 6:19, 20 says: "Ye are not your own, for ye are bought with a price: therefore glorify God in your body, and in your spirit, which are God's."

These words refer to each one of us. We have been bought with a price — the precious blood of Christ. Therefore we are not our own. It is strange how we will sing nostalgic words such as, "Now I belong to Jesus, Jesus belongs to me." Generally we are thinking of our own safety and security, of all that Jesus will do for me because He is my Savior. All the time we are telling the truth that "we belong to Jesus," we are not our own, but it is easier to overlook His ownership of us and to concentrate on all that we gain.

Notice how the verse in First Corinthians is underlining the words of the angel in Luke—there should be glory to God. See also that the glory is not only a spiritual response, but the verse says: "therefore glorify God in your body." Lordship will show not only in what I think and feel in a spiritual sense, but it will be seen in a physical sense. My body, its appearance, its actions, the places to which it goes, the friends with whom I meet, the books I read—and in a thousand other ways — this body will bring glory to God. This is not so in many of our lives. Our bodies are so often our own, to fulfill the desires of our hearts—good or bad. Only when I see myself belonging to Another, totally yielded to Him, seeking only to do His will—when the Shepherd is my Lord, as well as my Savior, only then will I know maximum success.

It is good to remind ourselves that the Lord-slave relationship with Christ is not designed to limit us, or to cramp our lives. Jesus said in Matthew 11:30: "For my yoke is easy, and my burden is light." He did not purchase us to make us suffer, to grind out His demands through our helpless lives. The will of God for us is always the love of God for us. God so loved . . . and He still does. Only when we yield to His Lordship do we experience the truth of those words: "Whose service is perfect freedom"—because true Lordship is based on love, a two-way love—His love for me and my responsive love for Him.

The third thing I want us to see in this Psalm is something I am calling "Maximum Separation." We saw, at the beginning of this chapter, the popularity of this Psalm. This is true, not only for the true believer, but also for the person who makes no real professions yet has a yearning after some diluted form of spiritual respectability. It is the kind of hymn popular with the occasional churchgoer. It is the kind of Psalm used in a funeral service, or a wedding service. It bring a comforting sense of well-being without making any demands upon the person's life.

I have heard people say: "It makes me feel good to hear the words read." All this is excellent, and we thank God for such an interest in the Word of God, but the tragedy is that many people use the Psalm who have no right to take it to themselves.

We should realize that just because a person says: "The Lord is my shepherd," that does not convey to him the blessings of the Psalm. Much repetition of the Psalm does not make it a reality. I could keep on saying repeatedly, "I am a millionaire," but the fact that I say it often enough does not make it true. I have to possess the resources to meet such a claim before I can say it and mean it.

The truth is, before I can say, "The Lord is my shepherd," and know it true in my heart, I must first of all say, "The Lord is my Savior." Before He can become my Shepherd, He must be my Savior. This involves a personal relationship at the cross, an acknowledgment and repentance of my sin, and a willingness to receive Christ into my heart and my life as my personal Savior.

This necessity to come and humble themselves is the greatest stumbling block to many people. They are happy to say, "The Lord is my shepherd," but they choose not to acknowledge Him as their Savior. You cannot have it one way only. It is either both, or nothing.

It can come as a shock to some people to see Psalm 23 as it applies to all those without Jesus as their Savior. If He is not their Savior, then He is not their Shepherd.

Thus it is the Psalm must begin:

> *The Lord is not my shepherd; I shall want.*
>
> *He maketh me not to lie down in green pastures: he leadeth me not beside the still waters.*
>
> *He restoreth not my soul: he leadeth me not in the paths of righteousness for his name's sake.*
>
> *Yea, though I walk through the valley of death, I will fear evil: for thou art not with me; thy rod and thy staff they comfort me not.*

Thou preparest not a table before me in the presence of mine enemies: thou anointest not my head with oil; my cup does not run over.

Surely goodness and mercy shall not follow me all the days of my life: and I will never dwell in the house of the Lord.

Just consider the bleak emptiness of verse 4 for the non-Christian. "Yea, though I walk through the valley of death, I will fear evil: for thou art not with me." What an awful, lonely experience that will be. For the Christian it is "the valley of the shadow of death." Remember that although shadows are dark, they never hurt anyone. It is only the shadow of death, the moment of darkness, then the miracle of glory. It is good to realize that you cannot have a shadow without a light, and, in one sense, the shadow of death is the result of the presence of the One who is the Light of the world. Jesus is there awaiting you. His own wonderful words in John 14:3 are: "And if I go and prepare a place for you, I will come again, and receive you unto myself; that where I am, there ye may be also."

What a glorious Shepherd, what safety, what a blessed hope is mine—if "The Lord is my shepherd." There may be someone reading these words who does not have this hope, this assurance. All you have is a cheerless present and a hopeless future. Why don't you make Him your Shepherd now? You have nothing to lose but your sin, your sorrow, and your emptiness. Why not come as a lost sheep seeking a good Shepherd? He said in John 6:37, "All that the Father giveth me shall come to me; and him that cometh to me I will in no wise cast out."

If you come you, too, will know maximum security. You can then go on to experience maximum success. You can leave forever the terrible separation and find the peace of God which passeth all understanding.

3

The Man Who Looked Four Ways

Psalm 73

There is something about Psalm 73 which makes it sound as if it was written especially for the present. It presents us with four pictures of the same man taken under four different sets of circumstances. Just as some people have graphic art hanging on their walls representing the four seasons, so this Psalm shows us, in a way, the four seasons in a person's experience.

In each case the man is looking out on life and, as he changes his aspect of looking, so his whole inward response is changed also. He is like many people today, looking and wondering and waiting. It would be good if you were to check yourself against this man. See how far you have looked and see if your reactions are the same as his.

The first look is found in verses 1-12. We could call this, "The Distressed Look." The Psalmist's eyes are on the world around him and all he sees causes him sorrow:

> *Truly God is good to Israel, even to such as are of a clean heart.*
>
> *But as for me, my feet were almost gone; my steps had well nigh slipped.*
>
> *For I was envious at the foolish, when I saw the prosperity of the wicked.*

For there are no bands in their death: but their strength is firm.

They are not in trouble as other men; neither are they plagued like other men.

Therefore pride compasseth them about as a chain; violence covereth them as a garment.

Their eyes stand out with fatness: they have more than heart could wish.

They are corrupt, and speak wickedly concerning oppression: they speak loftily.

They set their mouth against the heavens, and their tongue walketh through the earth.

Therefore his people return hither: and waters of a full cup are wrung out to them.

And they say, How doth God know? and is there knowledge in the most High?

Behold, these are the ungodly, who prosper in the world; they increase in riches.

The one topic of reference here is "they" and "them" and "their," as his eyes are on the ungodly. Fifteen times he uses the personal pronoun referring to the wicked. All that he says is true in his own experience, and amazingly it is true for today. The wicked still seem to prosper. They still have more than heart could wish. They are still corrupt and speak wickedly. In fact there is almost a direct reference to radio and television in verse nine: "They set their mouth against the heavens, and their tongue walketh through the earth." What a dramatic picture—the walking tongue!

The tragedy today is that corruption and wickedness is what often occupies the minds of many Christians. They feed on the newspapers with their lurid stories and on the TV with its pitiable procession of crime and rebellion. Their favorite topic of conversation is how bad the world is, and how much worse can it get, and that things were not like this in their day. All that they say is true, absolutely true. But, if this is where the eyes spend most of the time, and if the heart continues to worry over the wickedness around, then such a person becomes a useless negative character.

We should see these things and recognize them, but we should not be content with just the first look—"The Distressed Look."

The second look comes in verses 13-16. Here the writer has changed his point of interest from the world and the wickedness around him. He looks now within, and his mind is taken up with himself, his needs, and his problems. Notice the complete change in pronoun emphasis. In the first look it was all "they" and "them" and "their," now it is all "I" and "me."

> *Verily I have cleansed my heart in vain, and washed my hands in innocency.*
>
> *For all the day long have I been plagued, and chastened every morning.*
>
> *If I say, I will speak thus; behold, I should offend against the generation of thy children.*
>
> *When I thought to know this, it was too painful for me.*

If you count you will find that he uses the personal pronoun referring to himself nine times. This is a strong indication of where his interests lie. This second look we could call "The Disappointed Look." He has measured the wickedness in the world around him, he has seen the prosperity of those who live godless lives—and now he sees his own insecurity, his own insufficiency. He becomes sorry for himself and adopts a "poor me" attitude to life. He measures himself against a restless world, potent with increasing evil, and becomes crushed in his own soul.

The Bible would tell us to take a good look at ourselves and see if this is not often our own attitude to life. When I counsel with people in conferences and churches this is a common cause of Christian failure. So many people seem to spend their Christian life alternating from the "Distressed Look" to the "Disappointed Look." The increasing failure around them plus the increasing frustration within them wears them down, and wears them out.

There is an excellent illustration of this twofold experience in First Samuel 17. Here we read the story of Goliath, that monster of a man who terrorized the hearts of Saul and all his men. Verse 16 says: "And the Philistine drew near morning and evening, and presented himself forty days." For nearly six weeks the whole Israelite army had been brainwashed twice a day by this champion from Gath. He was a personification of the people we saw in the first part of Psalm 73. He set his mouth against the heavens, and spoke wickedly concerning oppression. Pride compassed Goliath about as a chain and violence covered him like a garment.

At the end of the forty days every heart in the army of Saul was crushed and disappointed. They were truly saying "poor me," because there seemed to be no possible hope of deliverance. Thus the two looks of this Psalm had taken their full effect.

Then David came on the scene. All these days the army had been cowering under the tongue of Goliath, David has been resting in the presence of God. He made inquiry as to the sudden retreat in verse 24: "And all the men of Israel, when they saw the man, fled from him, and were sore afraid." The terrified soldiers stammered out their fear and pointed to Goliath and said, in so many words, "Look at him! Have you seen him? What can we do? Look how much bigger he is than we are!" All that they said was true, every word of it, but their eyes were on their circumstances and on themselves.

Now hear the reply of David. They said, "Look how much bigger he is than we are!" David's attitude and reply was, "Yes, but look how much smaller he is than God!" They were both looking at the same situation, but one group was measuring the problem against their own human resources and quite naturally they saw no hope. David, fresh from the presence of God, saw the whole thing in a different light, and measured the great height of Goliath against the towering magnificence of Almighty God.

It is always sad to meet a Christian whose entire life is distressed and disappointed. Everyone of us can feel this way at times; the tragedy comes when these two looks become the basis of our Christian life and testimony. Do you have a Goliath in your life just now; some person, place, thing or situation from which you are daily running away? Why don't you go on with us now to see the other two looks, and to find all that God has for you in Christ?

The first two "looks" are definitely negative in cause and effect, the lost two "looks" become completely positive. The third look we can see from verses 17-22. It is here the writer gets his eyes off the world around, and the self within, and begins to see something of the majesty and holiness of God.

> *Until I went into the sanctuary of God; then understood I their end.*
>
> *Surely thou didst set them in slippery places: thou castedst them down into destruction.*
>
> *How are they brought into desolation, as in a moment! they are utterly consumed with terrors.*
>
> *As a dream when one awaketh; so, O Lord, when thou awakest, thou shalt despise their image.*
>
> *Thus my heart was grieved, and I was pricked in my reins.*
>
> *So foolish was I, and ignorant: I was as a beast before thee.*

See what a different look this is. I call this "The Discerning Look." The Psalmist is getting his eyes on God, and everything around him is beginning to make sense. God is still on the throne, and all that happens here is seen and noticed by Him. The boasting blasphemer and the proud, cruel person will some day come to a reckoning with God. Philippians 2:9-12 gives us God's last word concerning Christ:

Wherefore God also hath highly exalted him, and given him a name which is above every name:

That at the name of Jesus every knee should bow, of things in heaven, and things in earth, and things under the earth;

And that every tongue should confess that Jesus Christ is Lord, to the glory of God the Father.

So, in a definite way, the "Discerning Look" takes care of the first look, the "Distressed Look." There is an answer to the wickedness around.

But, how about the "Disappointed Look" within, the "poor me" attitude, this personal sense of present failure and need? It is good to know that someday God will have a glorious settling up of the world and its wickedness—but this, somehow, does not meet the immediate tension and frustration in the day-by-day life of the disappointed Christian.

It is just at this point that the reality of finding Jesus in the Psalms becomes a present blessing. We have already found the key from the words of the Lord Jesus: "All things must be fulfilled . . . in the psalms, concerning me." Now we can put the key into the closing verses of Psalm 73 and find wonderful and mighty words rich in blessing for the soul to whom the "Disappointed Look" is the daily image for living.

Undoubtedly the writer of Psalm 73 was expressing his own involvement with Jehovah God. Verses 23-28 tell of his joy and peace in the "God who is the strength of my heart, and my portion for ever." But, if we take a closer look at the words, we can begin to see that what is expressed here could only find its ultimate fulfillment in the risen, victorious Christ. Let us turn to those verses to find Jesus real to our own hearts:

Nevertheless I am continually with thee: thou hast holden me by my right hand.

Thou shalt guide me with thy counsel, and afterward receive me to glory.

Whom have I in heaven but thee? and there is none upon earth that I desire beside thee.

My flesh and my heart faileth: but God is the strength of my heart, and my portion for ever.

For, lo, they that are far from thee shall perish: thou hast destroyed all them that go a-whoring from thee.

But it is good for me to draw near to God: I have put my trust in the Lord God, that I may declare all thy works.

I am calling this look "The Delighted Look." Our eyes are on the Savior and we begin to see all that is ours, here and now, in Him. This is the answer to the second look, "The Disappointed Look," when the eyes were on self and the words "I" and "me" came so readily from the pen.

Look first at the opening words of verse 23: "Nevertheless I am continually with thee." This is a bold statement of definite assurance. Compare these words with the words of the Lord Himself in Matthew 28:20: "Lo, I am with you alway, even unto the end of the world." We believe the words of Christ. We are sure that He is with us always, as He promised. Then, if this is actually true, it follows automatically that I am continually with Him. These two statements become the two sides of the coin of comfort—He with me, I with Him. The strange thing is that there are many Christians who have accepted the words of Christ: "Lo, I am with you alway," as a belief in their mind, but it has never become real in their actual living.

I remember the words of a youth director at the end of a conference in his church. He was an ordained minister, well-trained in an evangelical seminary. When he stood up to give his own word of testimony he said, "I have learned this week that when Jesus said, 'Lo, I am with you alway,' He meant it. I have learned that Jesus is with me always."

See the beautiful significance of the end of verse 23.

"Thou hast holden me by my right hand." This is such a little phrase, yet one so full of great significance. I remember a lesson I learned when my children were small. There would be a young child upstairs asleep on a cot in the darkened room. Then something would disturb the little one, maybe a dream, and we would hear the cry of a troubled child echoing down the stairs. Quickly I would go to the room, but I would not put on the light, for that would wake the crying baby. I would draw near to the cot and take hold of a tiny hand. It was dark, no form could be seen, but the baby hand would hold fast to mine. Then, having found a source of comfort and strength, the crying would subside and the little one would slip again into the peacefulness of undisturbed sleep. There can be tremendous comfort for the troubled Christian who recognizes the presence of Christ as real, and even though it may be dark all around, he can reach out and find that "Thou has holden me by my right hand" is true.

Verse 24 is a simple pattern for daily living—being guided by His counsel—guided by the One who is always there, who will never leave me. I have this constant surety ahead of me, that He will "afterward receive me to glory." We live in a very impersonal world, where men become merely numbers in this computer age. It is good to know that He will receive me—it will be a personal reception from the Lord I love. I will not report at the office, at the gates of heaven, and have my card punched as I enter!

Verse 25 can become a tremendous treasury of truth if we look into it carefully. It speaks of a Person who is in heaven on my behalf, but, who, at the same time, is here also on earth, also on my behalf. How can this Person be in two places at the same time? This could be fulfilled only in the person of Christ. Look with me at First John 1:8-10. Here it speaks of the sin of the believer and how such sin can be both forgiven and cleansed.

John then continues: "My little children, these things write I unto you, that ye sin not. And if any man sin, we have an advocate with the Father, Jesus Christ the righteous: And he is the propitiation for our sins" (1 John 2:12).

This is telling of the work of Christ in heaven on our behalf. He is our Advocate, the attorney, the One who pleads our case before the Father.

Satan is the accuser of the brethren. We read in Revelation 12:9-11: "And the great dragon was cast out, that old serpent called the Devil, and Satan. . . . for the accuser of our brethren is cast down, which accused them before our God day and night. And they overcame him by the blood of the Lamb."

If ever Satan should accuse, the Lord Jesus is there as the Advocate. He does not excuse us our sin but, "He is the propitiation for our sins." This word "propitiation" means the mercy seat—the place where the blood was sprinkled as an atonement for sin. The blood of Jesus Christ is the answer not only for the sins of the sinner, but also for the sins of the saints.

We can truly say with the Psalmist: "Whom have I in heaven but thee?" We have a Savior who "is able also to save them to the uttermost that come unto God by him, seeing he ever liveth to make intercession for them" (Heb. 7:25). Jesus is always there, at the Father's right hand, our Advocate, ever living to make intercession for us. This is a tremendous thought and it should fill our hearts with great assurance and courage. This is not only good doctrine, it also is great reality.

But then the Psalmist continues in verse 25: "And there is none upon earth that I desire beside thee." The One who is in heaven on our behalf is also here on earth. How does this work out in the Bible? Look with me in John 14:15-20:

> *If ye love me, keep my commandments.*
> *And I will pray the Father, and he shall give*

you another Comforter, that he may abide with you for ever;

Even the Spirit of truth: whom the world cannot receive, because it seeth him not, neither knoweth him: but ye know him; for he dwelleth with you, and shall be in you.

I will not leave you comfortless: I will come to you.

Yet a little while, and the world seeth me no more; but ye see me: because I live, ye shall live also.

At that day ye shall know that I am in my Father, and ye in me, and I in you.

Here the Lord is speaking about a blessed person called the Comforter. He mentions the same person in verse 26: "But the Comforter, which is the Holy Ghost, whom the Father will send in my name." In John 15:26 the Lord Jesus said: "But when the Comforter is come, whom I will send unto you from the Father, even the Spirit of truth, which proceedeth from the Father, he shall testify of me." He made one more reference in John 16:7, 13, 14: "For if I go not away, the Comforter will not come unto you; but if I depart, I will send him unto you. . . . Howbeit when he, the Spirit of truth, is come, he will guide you into all truth: for he shall not speak of himself. . . . He shall glorify me."

Four times the Lord Jesus referred to the Comforter, the One who was to mean so much to us after He had gone. The interesting thing now is to look at the word "advocate" which we have just seen in First John 2:1. In the Greek that word was "parakletos"—one who comes alongside to help. We have a Parakletos in heaven, Jesus Christ the righteous. Now, if we look at the meaning of the word Comforter, we find that, in the Greek, that is also the word "parakletos."

So the Bible is teaching us that we have a Parakletos in heaven and a Parakletos on earth—just as Psalm

73:25 was saying: "Whom have I in heaven but thee? and there is none upon earth that I desire beside thee."

First John 2:1 says that the Parakletos is Jesus Christ the righteous. Now see what John 14 has to say about the Parakletos here on earth. The first clue comes in verse 16, where Jesus said: "he shall give you another Comforter." In the English language the word "another" has an inclusive meaning. It refers to "another" in number, that is, one more to what you already have. But in the Greek there are two different words, each one translated "another" in the English. There is an "another" of number — as in the usual English meaning. Then there is an "another" of the same kind. This second "another" indicates that the additional thing is the same as the other. It is this second "another" which is used in verse 16. Jesus was saying that the Father would give them a Parakletos who would be the same as Himself. That is why Jesus said in verse 17: "For he dwelleth with you, and shall be in you. I will not leave you comfortless [helpless]: I will come to you." He was going to leave His disciples, but He promised to return and dwell in them through the Parakletos.

Verse 26 says: "But the Comforter, which is the Holy Ghost, whom the Father will send in my name." Here we learn that the Holy Spirit was sent "in my name."

The word "name" in the Bible has a tremendous significance in this connection. It does not mean the five letters of the name of Jesus. John 20:31 says: "These are written, that ye might believe that Jesus is the Christ, the Son of God; and that believing ye might have life through his name." The words "his name" mean—"all that He is." We have life through all that He is—as He indwells us. Proverbs 18:10 says, "The name of the Lord is a strong tower: the righteous runneth into it, and is safe." The consistent teaching all through the Bible is that "the name" means "all that He is."

So we see in John 14:26 that the Comforter, who is also the Holy Spirit, has the work of making Jesus real in the heart and life of the believer. He is sent by the Father to be all that Jesus is. John 15:26 says "he shall testify of me." His work is to point to Jesus. John 16:13 says: "for he shall not speak of himself." This means, He shall not tell His own message. Verse 14 adds: "He shall glorify me."

Thus we see that the work of the Parakletos here on earth, the Holy Spirit, is to make Jesus real in our hearts and lives. His mission is not to speak of Himself or to glorify Himself, but to be in me all that Jesus is.

In one sense the Holy Spirit is Jesus Christ's other self. The Lord is in heaven as our Parakletos—our Advocate—and He is also here on earth indwelling us by His Holy Spirit.

This does not mean that the Holy Spirit is Jesus, or that Jesus is the Holy Spirit. This is part of the mystery of the Trinity—something we can never understand, something we are not expected to understand. There is God the Father, God the Son, and God the Holy Spirit. There are three Persons, but only one God.

We should never think that we can divide or separate the Trinity. There is a unity of persons with a division of ministry.

For example in John 14:23 Jesus said: "If a man love me, he will keep my words: and my Father will love him, and we will come unto him, and make our abode with him." Notice that not only is the believer indwelt by Christ, but also by the Father and the Spirit. Don't ever imagine that God the Father is in one place doing what He wants, and God the Son is in another place doing what He wants, while God the Spirit is in a third place busy about His own work. There is a consistent unity in the Godhead with an emphasis of persons in the ministry. In Second Corinthians 5:19 we read: "God was in Christ, reconciling the world unto Himself." In First John 3:16 we read: "Hereby perceive we the love of God, because he laid down his life for us."

Thus, the ministry of the Holy Spirit is to make Jesus real in our hearts and lives day by day. We can truly say that Jesus lives in us in the person of His Holy Spirit.

This is the whole significance of "The Delighted Look." This is why the fourth look is the complete answer to the second look of utter personal disappointment. We are nothing but failures, that is what the Bible teaches, and we always will be failures, for "they that are in the flesh cannot please God" (Rom. 8:8). But God has given us the answer to failure, a Savior who lives in our hearts and lives, ready to be Himself in us, if only we will step aside and let Him be the Lord of our Life, as we saw in Chapter 2 of this book.

This is the significance of Psalm 73:26: "My flesh and my heart faileth: but God is the strength of my heart, and my portion for ever." This could be true only in the risen, victorious, indwelling Christ. I can list and catalog all my failure and then I can say, "but God," and the whole picture can change as I rest in a Christ who is always there.

No wonder the Psalmist ends with the words: "But it is good for me to draw near to God." Have you seen the living Christ in this way?

He continues: "I have put my trust in the Lord God." Have you come to know the Lord Jesus in all His fullness—as the One who died for you on the cross to save you from your sins—then as the One who lives in your heart to save you from yourself, your failure, your fear? How far have you looked in the experience of this Psalm — distressed—disappointed—discerning —and now delighting in the Savior who ever lives in your heart?

Life is always radically and marvelously changed every time a Christian discovers Christ real in his heart and life.

4

The Sick Soul

Psalm 77

Psalm 73 was the picture of the man who looked four ways. Psalm 77 is the story of a man struggling with a load of problems, crying out to God in his anguish, and then finding the answer to his own need. This Psalm has something to say to every one of us. We could divide the first twelve verses into three separate sections—seeking, asking, finding.

Verses 1-6 present us with the picture of a man increasingly burdened with a load of undisclosed problems. We have no idea what his particular need was, we only see the effect of the pressure on his total emotional life:

> *I cried unto God with my voice, even unto God with my voice; and he gave ear unto me.*
>
> *In the day of my trouble I sought the Lord: my sore ran in the night, and ceased not: my soul refused to be comforted.*
>
> *I remembered God, and was troubled: I complained, and my spirit was overwhelmed.*
>
> *Thou holdest mine eyes waking: I am so troubled that I cannot speak.*
>
> *I have considered the days of old, the years of ancient times.*
>
> *I call to remembrance my song in the night: I commune with mine own heart: and my spirit made diligent search.*

Notice again the emphasis on the personal pronoun. Eighteen times in these six short verses he speaks of "I," "my," "me." His whole interest is wrapped up in the things which are beating him down. See the agony of soul as the words pour out: "I cried . . . I sought . . . I remembered . . . I complained . . . I am so troubled . . . I have considered . . . I call . . . I commune." Notice the pitiful phrase: "I am so troubled that I cannot speak."

There is something very relevant in these words. I meet people today who know the Lord as their personal Savior, but this is also their kind of language. There is almost a note of despair as such people pour out their problems. Even the telling of them opens again the wounds of deep sorrow. As in these six verses, there is a seeking for an unknown answer. In verses 7-9 the writer cries out six agonizing questions. This is the asking section. He is not asking the questions "to" God, but asking them "about" God. His voice rings out in the loneliness of empty fear:

> *Will the Lord cast off for ever? and will he be favorable no more? Is his mercy clean gone for evermore? doth his promise fail for evermore?*
>
> *Hath God forgotten to be gracious? hath he in anger shut up his tender mercies?*

Notice, he does not wait for an answer to any of his questions—he does not expect an answer. It is just the boiling over of the turmoil of verses 1-6. People still speak this way about God, talking about God behind His back. I remember a woman in Mount Hermon Conference, California, saying to me last year, "God has forgotten all about me. He doesn't know I even exist." I was struck with her bitter hopelessness, as if it didn't matter what she said about God, because He wasn't listening anyway.

But then the Psalmist found the answer to his own need. This, to me, is the significance of this Psalm. He did not remain under the burden of his sorrow; he found the way out. See how he handled the situation. The opening words of verse 10 show us the answer: "And I said, This is my infirmity." He took himself in hand, pulled himself together, almost shook himself, and said, "I am just a sick man. I need to handle this situation." He then went on to find the answer to his own failure and weakness. This answer came in a threefold repetition of the words: "I will remember." In verse 10 we read: "But I will remember the years of the right hand of the most High." Verse 11 continues: "I will remember the works of the Lord: surely I will remember thy wonders of old."

When I was studying this Psalm I was intrigued by this repetition, this trinity of remembrance. It seemed to have a familiar ring, this idea of remembering a thing three time to find the answer to a problem. Then I recalled some verses I had recently read in Second Peter 1. As I turned to the New Testament and read the words again I found once more the reality of the risen Christ as the only answer to the sorrows and heartaches of the downcast believer.

See this trinity of remembrance first in Second Peter 1:12: "Wherefore I will not be negligent to put you always in remembrance of these things." Then Peter goes on in the next verse: "to stir you up by putting you in remembrance." In verse 15 he adds these thoughtful words: "Moreover I will endeavour that ye may be able after my decease to have these things always in remembrance." How surprised Peter would have been if he could have known how far his words would reach, both in time and in distance.

This trinity of remembrance was also written to people in distress. Its whole purpose was to prepare them, and strengthen them as they moved on into certain suffering.

The background to Peter's letters is very significant. These messages were sent by the Holy Spirit to meet a number of needs in the early Church. Peter spoke of response to authority, inside and outside the church;

of relationship in the home, and the behavior of elders in the church. But he was also writing to prepare the hearts and minds of the believers for the terrible trouble that was creeping up on them.

On 19 July 64 there was a most destructive fire in the capital city of Rome. Legend has linked this fact with the story of Nero playing his violin. He has also been blamed for originating the devastating holocaust. There was an increasing outcry against such senseless destruction, and the people of Rome were looking for someone to blame. Rumors began to spread that this was the work of the people called Christians. Now the believers at this time were an unknown quantity. No one had ever seen their God, and their worship was not out in the open as with the pagan temples. They were a secret society who did strange things in unknown places. Gradually the rumors were believed and arrests among the Christians began to increase.

Nero, at this time, was given increasingly to acts of madness, and through him there developed the senseless and wicked persecution of the Christians. History records the sadistic and brutal acts that came as a result of this madness. When Nero saw that this persecution both delighted the common people and distracted their attention from other real areas of grievance, he stepped up the arrests and continued to provide free entertainment for the populace. Many believers, young and old, died in the arenas of the Roman world. Fiendish and devilish ways were devised to make the suffering of God's people more exciting and attractive.

As the program spread and developed, the need for more victims increased also. So it was there began a relentless "search and capture" program in many areas of the Roman empire. One of the reasons for Peter's letters was to prepare the hearts of the Christians as they awaited the approach of such bands of evil men. In First Peter 4:12, 13 he says: "Beloved, think it not strange concerning the fiery trial which is to try you, as though some strange thing happened unto you: But rejoice, inasmuch as ye are partakers of Christ's sufferings; that, when his glory shall be revealed, ye may be glad also with exceeding joy."

Remember that at this time the Christians did not have the New Testament as we have it today. The letters we possess in our Bible were still being written. It is easy to imagine what would be the scene when Peter's letters were first read. There must have been a time when a leader would come to his group, meeting in secret, with the first copy of Peter's second letter. Such a group would be apprehensive as they heard stories and rumors of the fate of other Christians. The arrival of a new letter from Peter would be a major occasion, and the simple believers would eagerly await the words. They would look for words of comfort, something that would instill new power and strength into their crowded and troubled lives.

As they listened to the reading of this second letter they may have been hoping for something new, some special significant word from God to meet their troubled souls—but instead of something new, God sent them this trinity of remembrance. As we have seen, three times Peter presses these words home to their hearts: "I will not be negligent to put you always in remembrance of these things." It is significant that in verse 12 he added: "though ye know them, and be established in the present truth." They had to remember what they had not forgotten. They had to remember that in which they were already firmly established.

Their one weapon of defense was to be "these things" to which Peter kept referring. The remembrance of "these things" — the practical application of "these things" in every walk of life, in every area of testing, was to be God's way of overcoming the evils and the terrors awaiting them. Just as in Psalm 77, the answer to the man's emotional problems was a remembrance of all that God had provided.

This is also God's answer to His people today — a

remembrance of "these things." There are many Christians who are like the people mentioned in Acts 17:21: "For all the Athenians and strangers which were there spent their time in nothing else, but either to tell, or to hear some new thing." As I meet and counsel with troubled Christians I sense, so often, a desire to reach beyond the Word of God. It is almost as if the Bible was all right for those people who lived long ago, but for ourselves, in our modern high pressure society, we need something new, something additional. This is surely why many believers are seeking new experiences, reading new books, following new names with the hope of finding an answer to the mounting pressures of our day.

God's word to us is still the same word that He sent through the pen of Peter—"remember these things."

It would be good for us then to look further into the letter and find out, for ourselves, what are "these things" to which the Holy Spirit directs our attention. See now with me the powerful arsenal of truth stored up in the first four verses of Second Peter:

> *Simon Peter, a servant and an apostle of Jesus Christ, to them that have obtained like precious faith with us through the righteousness of God and our Saviour Jesus Christ:*
>
> *Grace and peace be multiplied unto you through the knowledge of God, and of Jesus our Lord,*
>
> *According as his divine power hath given unto us all things that pertain to life and godliness, through the knowledge of him that hath called us to glory and virtue:*
>
> *Whereby are given unto us exceeding great and precious promises: that by these ye might be partakers of the divine nature, having escaped the corruption that is in the world through lust.*

These four verses contain tremendous and dynamic truth. This is where "these things" are clearly stated, to which Peter directed his trinity of remembrance. If these words were sufficient for the heroes of the early Church, surely they should contain a message for us today. We remember with awe the quality of lives these people lived. We recall with wonder and amazement the deaths that they died. Let us seek to discover the truths they believed and so find, for ourselves, the source of secret strength for our day of testing and brokenness.

The first great muscle of faith is seen in verse 2—the possibility of having grace and peace multiplied in our daily experience. These two blessed words—grace and peace—are very descriptive of what is missing in many Christians' lives. How much would you give, or sacrifice, for an absolute certain assurance of a precious inflow of grace and peace into your daily living? To know that this grace and this peace would multiply both in reality and in personal enjoyment — this seems beyond the wildest dreams of many people. They have accepted defeat as normal and their daily lives are dragged out in a pitiful demonstration of personal failure. And yet, God never saved you to be a failure. God never saved you to be washed up on the shores of heaven! He saved you at the cross so that: "Grace and peace might be multiplied unto you."

If this was God's purpose, then how do I begin to make it real in my life? The answer comes in the second half of verse 2, which should read: "through the increasing knowledge of God, and of Jesus our Lord." The key word here is "the increasing knowledge," not as stated in the King James Version, "the knowledge." Every true believer is saved by grace and, as they know God at the cross, so they have a sure peace in their hearts regarding their sins. Thus it is that "grace and peace" are ours at the cross, as we come to know the love of God set forth in the death of Christ.

The tragedy is that this is where many Christians stop in their knowledge of God and of Christ. They know they have peace with God through the death of Christ, and so they center their faith on the cross of

Christ. As the years go by they keep on looking back to the blessed experience they had when they came to know Jesus as their personal Savior. All this is absolutely right and true and proper, but you can be this kind of a Christian who looks back to the knowledge you had at the cross, and you can have a daily experience of Christian living which is full of failure and defeat. Why the defeat? Because you did not go on to "an increasing knowledge of God and of Christ."

God's total plan of salvation includes more than the death of Christ. Romans 5:10 assures us that being "reconciled to God by the death of his Son . . . we shall be saved by his life."

It is only when the Christian goes on to an increasing knowledge of God and of Christ, when he seeks to discover what additional blessing God has in the saving life of Christ—it is only then that the grace and the peace is multiplied.

Verse 3 tells us quite plainly that "his divine power hath given unto us all things that pertain unto life and godliness." Notice the words "all things"—these correspond to the "these things" referred to by Peter, which they were encouraged to remember. So here we find ourselves dealing with the vital realities.

The tenses in the Bible are always of significant value —see the tense in this verse: "His divine power hath given unto us." We already possess the "all things" because His divine power has already given them to us. We do not have to seek and wait and search for an additional "something," because we already have the "all things"!

Notice the purpose of these "all things" which we have received. It is all that we need for "life and godliness." "Life" is what I see and enjoy. "Godliness" is what the world sees when it looks at me. I have all I need for an inward and an outward witness, through these blessed "all things." Make sure you emphasize the word "all" in your daily experience. There are many Christians who live as if God has given them "some" of the things they need for life and godliness, and then they have to supply the rest. So their Christian life consists of a search for missing things that they must provide—more love, more grace, more kindness.

In trying to find these missing things they are caught up in an endless web of guilty endeavor. They will never find the missing things because they are not missing from our Christian lives. God gave us "all things" we need for life and godliness. We need to possess our possessions, and we do this by going on to an increasing knowledge of God and of Jesus our Lord.

The second half of verse 3 underlines again what we have already been discussing, that this experience of life and godliness comes "through the knowledge of him that hath called us to glory and virtue." See how the words "glory and virtue" match up with the words "life and godliness." As my knowledge of the saving life of Christ increases, and I come, more and more, to recognize His indwelling presence by His Holy Spirit, then the truth of Colossians 1:27 becomes real in my own experience: "which is Christ in you, the hope of glory." As the life of Christ is made manifest through my mortal flesh, so the glory of Christ will be seen, known and experienced.

In like manner the words godliness and virtue equate themselves, and that which is seen by the world around is the godliness resulting from the presence of the Son of God, and the virtue is His own blessed life lived out through me. This is what the Holy Spirit was telling these dear people through the pen of Peter—"remember these things," and you have the answer to living, and dying.

5

The One Answer to Everything

Psalm 77

So far in these few verses of Second Peter we have made mention of six blessed experiences — grace and peace, life and godliness, glory and virtue. They are six precious jewels to whet the appetite of every earnest, seeking Christian. Now, as we go on to verse 4, we touch the living heart of these precious truths. Let us keep on reminding ourselves that these are "these things" which the Holy Spirit is spotlighting as the only answer to suffering and testing. It is all good theology and it makes the backbone to all good doctrine, but, it is more than abstract truth.

This is the stuff to live with, and die with. This is what turns boys into men, and men into heroes. This is the muscle fiber of the Christian faith. Without it there will be a flabby softness which possesses no capacity to live the life God intended us to live. With these truths integrated into our innermost beings we, too, can go on to be the same kind of people whose lives challenged the decadent world of Rome and whose deaths brought honor and glory to the Lord they loved.

Verse 4 is the climax to this section of truth. See again those key words: "Whereby are given unto us." Notice the same tense once more, the present tense. These things "are" given, we already possess them, we do not have to search for another experience.

See also the repetition of the word "given." It comes in verses 3 and 4. Everything comes as a free gift from God our Father. He is the giver of every good and perfect gift. We do not earn anything, or merit anything. We are not worthy of anything, nor do we deserve anything—it is all the gift of God.

It is worth reminding ourselves at this time that we were created to receive. Just as God is the great Giver, so we were created to be complementary to the act of giving. We fit into God's pattern of performance only as we continue to receive—in all areas. The bodies we now possess are the result of the food we have received throughout our lives. The skills and knowledge we now possess are the result of the education we have received. The salvation we now enjoy is ours only because we have received that which God gave — "God so loved the world, that he gave his only begotten Son"—"the gift of God is eternal life."

If we continue to receive from God, then we continue in the pattern that He established. But, when we stop being receivers and start being producers, then we run into real trouble.

This is the problem with many earnest believers. When they were babes in Christ they were, of necessity, totally dependent on Christ. Because of their dependence, their lives were thriving, glowing examples of Christian living and witnessing. It was at such a period in their lives that they had the most joy and the most success. But then, as time passed, they gradually ceased to be so dependent on Christ. They assumed that as they became older and more mature in the faith so they should take on more responsibility and, as a result, instead of continuing to receive from Christ, they started to promote, produce and show their own innate ability in action. Once this attitude becomes firmly fixed, then the quality of real Christian living begins to deteriorate. The believer becomes the originator of his own life and program. As areas of failure reveal themselves, so he tries all the harder to live the Christian life. Guilt follows hard on failure, and these two miserable experiences become the daily ingredient of the failing Christian life. These are the antithesis of the "life and godliness" we read of in verse 3 — the all things given to us by God.

So verse 4 tells us that all these things are the "exceeding great and precious promises" which are given to us. Notice the extravagance of language that seeks to measure the promises of God. The promises of God are the realities of God. We make promises in all sincerity, but we do so conscious of the fact that often they never become real. Our promises always have reservations, and no one is ever surprised when he finds it impossible to fulfill his hopes and aspirations. But this is never so with God. See the assurance of this fact from the Word of God: "there hath not failed one word of all his good promise, which he promised by the hand of Moses his servant" (1 Kings 8:56). "He staggered not at the promise of God through unbelief; but was strong in faith, giving glory to God; And being fully persuaded that, what he had promised, he was able also to perform" (Rom. 4:20, 21).

This is what made Abraham so great, why he became the friend of God—his total dependence on the promises of God. Abraham was fully persuaded that, what God had promised, He was able to fulfill, and so he continued to receive from God in all areas.

Abraham certainly received great promises and he lived in the good of them, but this fourth verse is telling us the greatest, the most wonderful, the most incredible promise God ever made—and He made it to us—"that ye might be partakers of the divine nature."

I remember the first time I met that phrase years ago. I was in a Bible study and the speaker was reading the first chapter of Second Peter. As I listened to his voice this phrase, in verse 4, struck home to my heart. I suppose I had read it before, although nothing had ever previously registered in my mind. But at that moment I was jolted out of my complacency. I suddenly heard that I was a partaker of the divine nature. I suddenly realized that Jesus actually indwelt me. I tingled with awe and wonder. I already had my own human nature—feeble and fallen—and to think that when I became a Christian I received a new nature—the life of Christ Himself. That moment marked a turning point in my Christian life.

Has it ever struck home to you that you, too, are a partaker of the divine nature? Have you ever accepted the challenge that all "these things" are yours now because Christ indwells you? Do you begin to realize that the grace and peace, the life and godliness, the glory and virtue, and a host of other blessed vital experiences are now within your grasp because you are a partaker of the divine nature?

This was the whole point of the Spirit's message to the needy people of Peter's day. They did not need some new truth, some new ability. They had all things in Christ. This possession was not just a theory, a doctrine, and an article of belief; it was the very core of Christian living. In just the same way this is God's gift to us in our own day and generation.

We do not need new experiences, new truths, new ideas. We already have all things in Christ. Our greatest need is to get into gear with God, to let out the clutch of faith and to allow the driving power of the indwelling Christ to mesh with the machinery of our little lives. Or, to turn from the mechanical to the miraculous, to stagger "not at the promise of God through unbelief; but [to be] strong in faith, giving glory to God; [to be] fully persuaded that, what he [has] promised, he [is] able also to perform" (Rom. 4:20).

Thus it was, in Peter's day, that the Holy Spirit spoke to the needy, the fearful and the bewildered people of God. Verses 1-4 outline, as we have just seen, the rich abundant source of blessing which is resident in the heart and life of each believer through the indwelling Christ. But the challenge through Peter does not stop there. Verses 1-4 outline what God has provided, verses 5-7 go on to tell our part in this trinity of remembrance.

Verse 5 begins with these significant words: "And besides this"—thus underlining that there is something else equally necessary in my daily experience. This fact needs to be emphasized again and again. There is a quality of faith which listens to the first four verses and then says, in so many words, "Thank You, Lord Jesus, for all You have done. Thank You. You dwell in my heart and now I can just sit back and rest, and leave it all to You. It is all in Your hands. I'm going to relax and do nothing. If anything goes wrong, don't blame me—I've committed it all to You!" I know this is a deliberate overstatement and no one would actually say these words—or would they?

Verses 5-7 tell what we need to do in this adventure of faith — we are told to add to our faith certain qualities. It makes an interesting contrast to see that in verse 2 God does the multiplying, but in verse 5 we have to do the adding:

> *And beside this, giving all diligence, add to your faith virtue; and to virtue knowledge;*
>
> *And to knowledge temperance; and to temperance patience; and to patience godliness;*
>
> *And to godliness brotherly kindness; and to brotherly kindness charity.*

There are thus seven things we have to add, or seven areas of our lives that must be involved with the precious promises, if we are to be all that God would have us be in our day of testing.

A modern translation would tell us to employ every effort to add to our faith energy, and to our energy intelligence, to our intelligence self-control, to our self-control endurance, and to our endurance piety. To our piety we add brotherly kindness and the culminating factor is the addition of Christian love. This presents a wonderful sevenfold involvement with the indwelling

Christ. It touches on every facet of personality and character, and challenges us to go on more and more to total involvement.

When I add my energy, I cancel out any laziness. I see the words of Paul in Colossians 1:29 (Amplified): "For this I labor [unto weariness], striving with all the superhuman energy which He so mightily enkindles and works within me." This is a perfect example of what Peter has been describing. Here is no laziness, no standing back while Jesus does it all. To use the words of Winston Churchill, it is adding "Blood, toil, tears and sweat" in the service of the Lord. My blood if needs be, my toil, my tears and my sweat—as He works on in my yielded life.

To this energy I add my intelligence. This is an excellent, satisfying thought. When I become a Christian I do not lose my intelligence. I do not abdicate the area of intellectual ability to become a spiritual moron. All the intelligence I have is added to the energy I possess—for Christ to use as He thinks best.

Then to my intelligence I add self-control, so that never once do I overstep the bounds of my natural God-given ability. This is so necessary. The highly intelligent person can so easily succumb to the temptation of going it alone, of giving full rein to his natural abilities so that self takes over in an unusual way. Self-control cuts me down to size as I measure myself against the Son of God who loved me and gave Himself for me.

To my self-control I bring endurance — the ability to go on beyond the normal human barrier of ease and comfort. The human capacity for endurance is seen in all walks of life and under the most trying circumstances. It reaches its greatest heights when it is added to the reality of the indwelling Christ.

The next addition is godliness or piety. This is a much outmoded idea these days when the overriding factor is to be yourself. And yet this was the aim of Paul as he told it in Second Corinthians 4:10 and 11:

"that the life also of Jesus might be made manifest in our body [mortal flesh]." When the life of the indwelling Christ shines through the veil of mortal flesh then we see true godliness and piety. We do not look for an implicit obedience to a legalistic plan for living, but for the sweet outflowing of the life of Him who was meek and lowly in heart.

What follows next will be the natural outcome — brotherly kindness and real Christian love. It is really interesting to note that Christian love, as detailed here, is the outcome of a sevenfold involvement with Christ. It is not a vacant, flabby, ephemeral experience built on nothing, but the result of a deliberate building up of energy plus intelligence, plus self-control, plus endurance, plus godliness, plus real brotherly kindness. This kind of love has hands and feet and muscles. This does not breathe sweet nothings, but gets down to where the action is. It knows how to weep and share and sacrifice.

This then is what the Holy Spirit brought through the pen of Peter to people who were facing the horror of a mad, besotted Roman world. They were to keep on receiving all that God had for them in Christ, and to Him they had to add and yield all that they possessed, for His glory. It is to this that Peter was pointing when he brought his trinity of remembrance: "Wherefore I will not be negligent to put you always in remembrance of these things, though ye know them, and be established in the present truth." This was God's answer to the sick soul in the New Testament days, just as we saw the answer in Psalm 77.

There are two more verses we must consider. Verses 8 and 9 paint two pictures that illustrate so clearly what is the result if these precious things are not fulfilled in our hearts and lives.

Verse 8 says: "For if these things be in you, and abound, they make you that ye shall neither be barren nor unfruitful in the knowledge of our Lord Jesus Christ." This verse is showing us that it is possible to have a limited knowledge of our Lord Jesus Christ, which can still leave us barren and unfruitful in our daily lives. Notice that the words say "barren nor unfruitful in the knowledge." Some people are barren and unfruitful because of their ignorance; these are so because of their knowledge. This takes us back to verse 2, once more, where we saw the possibility of grace and peace being multiplied through the increasing knowledge of God, and of Jesus our Lord. As we go on in the teaching we have already covered, then the prospect of barrenness and unfruitfulness disappears.

Verse 9 tells us, again referring to "these things": "But he that lacketh these things is blind, and cannot see afar off, and hath forgotten that he was purged from his old sins." Here is the condition of the Christian who is not living in the good of these two sections of truth—he is blind. The word used here for "blind" is a special word which paints a vivid illustration. It does not mean to be without sight. The actual meaning is, "to be blinkered." This refers to blinkers which are part of the head-harness of a horse. They are the two rectangular pieces of leather which line up on each side of the horse's head, alongside the eyes. Their purpose is to limit the vision of the animal. Without blinkers the horse has a full constant 180° vision. The animal can thus be much distressed and alarmed with what it sees, especially if it is an area of much noise and activity. The blinkers serve as a means of cutting off the unpleasant and the disturbing. By closing the blinkers the horse sees less and less.

What an amazing picture of a Christian living in a broken, needy world, with all the sights and sounds of sin and suffering around him, but he has no true realization of the indwelling Christ, he has not claimed the precious promises, he has not added his personal involvement to the concern of Christ and so he is blinkered. The needs and the problems are all around him, but he closes the blinkers so that nothing will disturb him in his world of mediocre insufficiency.

These are powerful challenges from the Word of God. They were meant to move God's people to action, in Peter's day. Here was the answer both to fear and complacency. They are still God's challenge to us today. God has nothing new to offer—only the glorious, wonderful presence of Christ indwelling us. As we claim His promises, recognize His presence, and add our total involvement then we, too, will find the answer to our sickness and our stagnation. There is no alternative to Christ. It is either this that we have studied—or nothing!

Remember—we are finding the living Christ in the Psalms. Our search is taking us from the Old Testament to the New Testament. The beginning of the suggestion of blessing in Psalm 77 . . . "I will remember" has led us to the glorious fulfillment in Second Peter 1 . . . "These things always in remembrance." How good it is to know and appropriate Him of whom it is said: "Jesus Christ the same yesterday, and today, and for ever" (Heb. 13:8).

6

The Source of Rest

Psalm 116

You will remember that we are taking time to look into the Psalms, because Jesus said we would find Him there. He gave this promise in Luke 24:44 as He appeared and spoke to His own in all His risen power. This promise has become our key with which we can unlock the doors of truth and find a new relevance to Christ, a new setting forth of His person and His work, and a new source of challenge and blessing to our own hearts.

Psalm 116 has long been a joy to my heart. The first words echo the language of my love to my Lord:

> *I love the Lord, because he hath heard my voice and my supplications.*
>
> *Because he hath inclined his ear unto me, therefore will I call upon him as long as I live.*
>
> *The sorrows of death compassed me, and the pains of hell gat hold upon me: I found trouble and sorrow.*
>
> *Then called I upon the name of the Lord: O Lord, I beseech thee, deliver my soul.*
>
> *Gracious is the Lord, and righteous; yea, our God is merciful.*
>
> *The Lord preserveth the simple: I was brought low, and he helped me.*

Surely this is the language of every redeemed heart. It tells forth in beautiful words the story of our own personal experience with Christ, when we come to Him with all our sin and need and He delivered our souls. This is recounting the past blessing in our life, what He did for us, perhaps years ago. All true believers can look back to such a day, and, as they do so, the same words return to their lips: "I love the Lord, because he hath heard my voice and my supplications."

But the Psalmist is not concerned only with the past experience; he moves on in verses 7-9 to the setting forth of a present blessing. It is in these verses we can begin to find the risen Christ in a new way:

> *Return unto thy rest, O my soul; for the Lord hath dealt bountifully with thee.*
>
> *For thou hast delivered my soul from death, mine eyes from tears, and my feet from falling.*
>
> *I will walk before the Lord in the land of the living.*

Verse 7 is very significant. It says: "Return unto thy rest, O my soul." This is spelling out the condition of many believers. They have a past blessing, but they have lost a present rest. This is the whole point of this Psalm. The writer can look back to what God has done in the past—that is good and wonderful—but he needs something now for the present. He needs to recapture the rest that once filled his soul with peace and joy. Maybe this is your special need—to find rest in the midst of life's struggle and turmoil. I hear people talking about living on their nerves, of struggling to keep up with the increasing pace of life and the increasing pressures. It is true that our lives are under great pressure, that we are living in times of unusual tension, but the fact remains that there is "rest" for the people of God. Hebrews 4:9 tells us: "There remaineth therefore a rest to the people of God."

This is not some theoretical, theological, vague entity, but an actual glorious reality. It is this we are looking for as we open the door of this Psalm. Why is it that so many Christians miss the rest which God has promised? Hebrews 3:19 gives one answer, with reference to the children of Israel: "So we see that they could not enter in [his rest] because of unbelief." It was just plain unbelief that kept them out of the rest God had promised. Hebrews 4:1, 2 has words which could apply directly to us in our present discussion: "Let us therefore fear, lest, a promise being left us of entering into his rest, any of you should seem to come short of it.

"For unto us was the gospel preached, as well as unto them: but the word preached did not profit them, not being mixed with faith in them that heard it."

Here is another reason for failure to find the rest God has promised—they did not use faith! They heard all the promises, understood all the instructions, but they failed to add the missing ingredient—their own simple faith.

All this is true of many of us today. There are some Christians who do not believe that there is such a thing as rest. Their idea of living the Christian life is struggling, failing, struggling once more, and battling on until, finally, they reach Canaan's happy shore. They never enter into rest, because of their unbelief.

There are others, many of them timid souls, who believe there *is* such a thing as "resting in Christ." They study the Scriptures and read the right books but when it comes to stepping out and making an actual decision to yield to Christ, they draw back. They have all the correct ingredients for a blessed experience with Christ, but they fail to add the one contribution that would make it real—they do not mix it with their own childlike faith. So they fail to enter into rest because of indecision.

But let us get back to Psalm 116:7 nd see the truth of rest as it unfolds before our eyes. We are thinking in this chapter of the source of rest, and here in verse 7 we see it being spelled out: 'Return unto thy rest, O my soul; for the Lord hath dealt bountifully with thee." The source of all rest is the bountiful blessing that comes from God. The key word here is "bountifully"—an overflowing abundance of blessing that has come from God. How much have you been involved in the overflowing abundance? Lack of involvement means lack of rest.

Then, in an unusual way, verse 8 goes on to tell of the bountiful dealing of God: "For thou hast delivered my soul from death, mine eyes from tears, and my feet from falling." Here we have, in simple graphic words, the three tenses of our salvation—the past, the future and the present tense, in that order. This is the Gospel with which we need to mix our faith in order to find the rest of God.

See the beautiful way in which the past tense of our salvation is described: "Thou hast delivered my soul from death." Ephesians 2:1 gives us the same thing in New Testament language: "And you hath he quickened, who were dead in trespasses and sins." We were sinners, and, because of that, we were dead. We were on our way to a lost eternity, but He saved us, delivered us from the awfulness of death. We were born again—we received new life. This is what He has done for us. This is the past tense of our salvation. This is the foundation of present rest, but, by itself, it is not sufficient.

The next phrase goes on to speak of the future tense of our salvation: "Thou hast delivered . . . mine eyes from tears." Have you ever seen a pagan funeral? It is on such an occasion that the hopelessness of death stands out in all its fear and agony and total emptiness. The mourners are grieving for the loss of their loved one, but at the same time they are terrified of his spirit. His body they can bury, but his spirit can turn against them and harm them. And so you hear the wails and screams and see the tears—a vivid mixture of sorrow, fear, distress, loneliness, anxiety.

These are the extremes of pagan reaction, but even in so-called civilized countries there is a sense of hopelessness in the funeral of a non-Christian. Brave words may be spoken as the character of the deceased is built up before the mourners, but it is all built on a hopeless nothing. The tears that are shed are tears of finality and futility.

How different with the believer: "Thou hast delivered . . . mine eyes from tears." True, there are the natural tears that come because of the moment of separation, but there is also the blessed hope that this is not the end. Death has lost its sting and the grave has lost its victory—in Christ. We know whom we have believed, we know that our Redeemer lives and we have the certain assurance that this is not the end. So by the bountiful dealing of our heavenly Father we have been redeemed, we have our sins forgiven and we have a home in heaven.

Wonderful as these two gifts are, they are not sufficient of themselves to provide that sure sense of rest to which our thoughts are turning in this chapter. Every true Christian believes in these two gifts of God. This is what many people refer to when they speak of being saved. But there are many believers who are confident in these two areas, who are still without a real sense of rest. How is this possible in a Christian's experience? The answer is really very simple — they have not appropriated all that God has given in His bountiful dealings.

There is still one more phrase in verse 8, which covers one more area of Christian experience: "Thou hast delivered . . . my feet from falling" This refers to the present tense, to my life as I live it out day by day. God has provided a way whereby the Christian can be daily delivered. Romans 5:10 (Amplified) says: "For if while we were enemies we were reconciled to God through the death of His Son, it is much more [certain], now that we are reconciled, that we shall be saved [daily delivered from sin's dominion] through His [resurrection] life."

Reconciliation includes the past and the future tenses of salvation — sins forgiven, and a home in heaven. Both of these are mine because Jesus died for me. But this verse is telling me that I can be daily delivered by His resurrection life. This was the culminating gift of a bountiful God. He sent His Son, not only to die for me on the cross, but He sent Him also to indwell me by His Holy Spirit.

When I make Jesus real in my life at the cross, accepting Him as my personal Savior, then I am reconciled. When I go on to make Him real in my life, day by day, appropriating all that He is for all that I need, then I can have the blessed, glorious experience of being daily delivered. He can keep my feet from falling — falling into sin and temptation, falling into fear and anxiety, falling into laziness and deadness.

This threefold involvement with the Lord Jesus is the source of rest. This rest can become a reality when I do what we saw in Hebrews, when I mix it with faith. Remember faith is two empty hands stretched out to take what God offers. As I receive and say "Thank You, Lord Jesus," then I can begin to enter into my rest. I rest in all that He is for all that I need.

Verse 9 follows on so beautifully: "I will walk before the Lord in the land of the living." When my feet have been delivered from falling, then I can begin to walk. There is one other point we need to realize at this time. I have heard Christians speak of "taking the step of faith." By this they refer to the act of trusting Christ as their Savior. The step of faith describes their involvement with Christ at the cross. This is a simple and a beautiful illustration, but it can lead to failure in daily living. If all I have taken is "a step of faith" then I am not qualified to live the Christian life day by day. Verse 9 says, "I will walk before the Lord in the land of the living." Walking is a series of steps, not just one step alone. This is exactly what the Christian life is — a walk that consists of a series of steps of faith. I take the initial step in the saving death of Christ, but this has to be followed by a series of steps of faith in the saving life of Christ. Jesus said in John 14:19: "Because I live, ye shall live also." As I rest in His saving life so I begin to live, and I can truly walk in the land of the living.

This same truth is brought out in Colossians 2:6: "As ye have therefore received Christ Jesus the Lord, so walk ye in him." I began my Christian life by receiving Christ Jesus the Lord—at the cross. In just the same way I continue my Christian life, receiving Christ Jesus—appropriating all that He is for all that I need. I walk, receiving Jesus—the walk of faith. In this way, once more, I can walk before the Lord in the land of the living.

This is the source of rest—when you mix with it your simple, childlike faith.

7

The Secret of Rest

Psalm 116

It is a wonderful thing to come to grips with the reality of rest in the daily life of the believer. We have seen that this is a possibility through the bountiful provision of God. The total provision of God in a threefold experience of salvation is the basis for daily rest and peace, for joy and victory.

In this chapter we will use the key of faith again, and go on through other doors to find what is the secret of rest, to discover what we must do to make this rest a living reality in our own daily experience.

Psalm 116:12-18 contains a real treasure chest full of precious jewels from the Lord:

> *What shall I render unto the Lord for all his benefits toward me?*
>
> *I will take the cup of salvation, and call upon the name of the Lord.*
>
> *I will pay my vows unto the Lord now in the presence of all his people.*
>
> *Precious in the sight of the Lord is the death of his saints.*
>
> *O Lord, truly I am thy servant; I am thy servant, and the son of thine handmaid: thou hast loosed my bonds.*
>
> *I will offer to thee the sacrifice of thanksgiving, and will call upon the name of the Lord.*
>
> *I will pay my vows unto the Lord now in the presence of all his people.*

Verses 7-9 spoke of the bountiful provision made by God for our salvation, and for our enjoyment of rest. Verse 12 asks the simple questions: "What can I do, what can I give to God in response to such a bountiful provision?" The rest of this section goes on to tell three things that we can do in response to the three areas of blessing God has provided for us.

Verse 13 describes the first thing the sinner must do as he turns to God in gratitude: "I will take the cup of salvation, and call upon the name of the Lord." God offers to every sinner the cup of salvation, but He can do this only because of what the Lord Jesus has done.

If we turn back to Psalm 75:8 we see a reference to another cup: "For in the hand of the Lord there is a cup, and the wine is red; it is full of mixture; and he poureth out of the same: but the dregs thereof, all the wicked of the earth shall wring them out, and drink them." Notice where the cup is — in the hand of the Lord — and He is going to present it to the wicked of the earth. This is the cup of judgment, God's judgment on sin and all unrighteousness. This is the cup that you and I should drink. We are the sinners and this is the sinner's cup.

But look now with me in Matthew 26:36-42. Here we find the story of Jesus in the Garden of Gethsemane. He left His disciples to watch with Him, while He went and bowed in prayer before His Father. Verse 39 says: "And he went a little farther, and fell on his face, and prayed, saying, O my Father, if it be possible, let this cup pass from me: nevertheless not as I will, but as thou wilt." Verse 42 tells how "He went away again the second time, and prayed, saying, O my Father, if this cup may not pass away from me, except I drink it, thy will be done."

Have you ever wondered what cup it was about which Jesus was praying? It was the cup of judgment detailed in Psalm 75. God was finding an answer to His righteous judgment on sin. Paul said in Galatians 2:20: "The Son of God, who loved me, and gave himself for me." That is exactly what Jesus did for you and for me. It was our cup of judgment—we were the sinners, but Jesus faced the drinking of this awful cup in the Garden and He drained the last drops on Calvary's cross.

Now notice the amazing love of God, poured out in all His bounteous giving. Not only did Jesus drink the cup of judgment on our behalf, but God now goes one stage farther and offers to us the cup of salvation—what amazing grace!

The Psalmist asked his question, "What shall I do in return?" He answered his own question by saying, "I will take the cup of salvation." This is the first thing we must do when we come to God as sinners seeking His forgiveness. It is really a strange situation—almost as if we were doing God a favor by taking this blessed cup, and yet there are many people who refuse to take the cup so offered. By refusing the cup, they throw the love of God back where it came from. For those who refuse the cup of salvation there remains but the awful and holy judgment of God.

There is one more cup we can think of. This also is offered to us from the hand of God. Paul describes it for us in First Corinthians 11:23-26:

> *For I have received of the Lord that which also I delivered unto you, That the Lord Jesus the same night in which he was betrayed took bread:*
> *And when he had given thanks, he brake it, and said, Take, eat: this is my body, which is broken for you: this do in remembrance of me.*
> *After the same manner also he took the cup, when he had supped, saying, This cup is the new testament in my blood: this do ye, as oft as ye drink it, in remembrance of me.*
> *For as often as ye eat this bread, and drink this cup, ye do shew the Lord's death till he come.*

This is the blessed cup of remembrance. This cup, in a way, is the outcome of the other two cups. The cup of judgment and the cup of salvation are united as we take the cup of remembrance. When we partake of the Lord's Supper we recall the fact that we were the sinners, that to us belongs the cup of judgment. Then we consider the price that Jesus paid. We meditate on His sufferings. We recall again the majestic mercy of God in offering to us the cup of salvation. When our hearts are full of true worship and adoration, then we take the cup of remembrance. As we drink it we can feel in our hearts a full response to the words of the Psalm: "What shall I render unto the Lord for all his benefits toward me?

"I will take the cup of salvation, and call upon the name of the Lord." To these words we couple the blessed words of our Savior: "This do in remembrance of me." How gladly we take the cup of remembrance in response to His invitation.

Having taken the cup of salvation as detailed in verse 13, we then go on to do what is recorded in verse 14: "I will pay my vows unto the Lord now." Notice that the words are, "I will *pay* my vows." I have found that some Christians are often more ready to *make* vows unto the Lord. They may be in a meeting where the Spirit is moving mightily and a challenge is given to step out for the Lord, to yield to Him, to commit to Him in whatever way is asked. At such times there are those whose hearts are moved, especially among young people, and we see them taking a stand for God, committing their lives to Him as they have been asked. In one sense, they are making a vow before the Lord, they are promising to do certain things, or to follow certain lines of response. It all looks wonderful as they stand there making their vows. Others in the gathering look at them with admiration and even with envy. They become the center of attraction while the service lasts. But, at the end of the service, when it is all over, experience teaches that some who made the vows go home and soon forget all that was transacted that night.

Experience also shows that the same thing can happen repeatedly. Once more the challenge is given, once more they move forward to make wonderful vows to God. Once more the vows become forgotten memories in the busy rush of life.

See now the challenge behind the words in verse 14: "I will pay my vows unto the Lord now." This is not a case of making new vows, but of paying the vows already made on previous occasions.

I have found that this is why some Christians never find real rest. God spoke to them one day. They heard His voice, and they knew what He meant. They responded to God in words of earnest submission. They made their vow—and that was all that came of it. They have never paid the vow that they made.

If all the vows made by earnest Christians were paid to God there would be a significant change in the Church today. There would be no empty places on the mission fields of the world. There would be no closing down of vital work because of insufficient financial support. There would be many more Christian homes where the family altar was raised each day, more time spent in prayer and Bible study, more love shown to others. So much more would come alive and effective if Christians paid the vows they have already made.

There may be someone reading these words now to whom the Spirit of God is saying, "This is you. This is what you have done. This is why you have no real rest in your heart." May I suggest that you bring the whole thing before the Lord, and seek His will and His mind on the situation. If it is impossible now to pay your vow, then seek His forgiveness and His cleansing. It may be that God still needs your response. In any case do not dismiss the matter. Deal with it thoroughly so that you can find rest.

The Bible has some straight speaking for those who find it easy to make vows, and then just as easy to forget what was said. Ecclesiastes 5:4 says: "When thou vowest a vow unto God, defer not to pay it; for he hath no pleasure in fools: pay that which thou hast vowed." Verses 5 and 6 follow this with this good advice: "Better is it that thou shouldest not vow, than that thou shouldest vow and not pay. Suffer not thy mouth to cause thy flesh to sin."

These are very pointed words—it is far better not to make a vow, than to give way to an emotional moment of making a vow which is never fulfilled. How easily we can delude ourselves into thinking that fine words, emotionally spoken, will impress the heart of God—suffer not thy mouth to cause thy flesh to sin!

When we turn our attention next to Psalm 116:15, there seems to be no connection whatever between the thought of paying a vow and what is recorded in these words: "Precious in the sight of the Lord is the death of his saints." Have you ever felt that this verse was out of place in this psalm? I know we use the words at a funeral service, finding comfort in the thoughts expressed therein, but this psalm is not talking about funerals, it is dealing with the vital subject of finding rest through response to the bountiful provision of God.

This verse is telling the third thing we must do if we wish to make a threefold response to the threefold offer of God's salvation. We will understand it better if we realize that there is another word we can use instead of "precious." This verse can say: "*Valuable* in the sight of the Lord is the death of his saints." Forget the idea of funerals and burial and see that these words have something tremendous to say to each one of us—it is of value to God when we die and get ourselves out of the way.

The greatest barrier to the fulfillment of God's richest blessing in our lives is not our circumstances but ourselves. We are our own worst enemies. We, through our continued ignorance of God's will, plan and scheme, act and re-act as dictated by our own will. Sometimes our failure is in our sin, often in our service. We take off on some busy act of service for God, inspired by our own ideas and motivated by our own enthusiasm —and, time and again, it all ends up in failure.

God could do a much better job if we would only desist from helping Him. This is exactly what this verse is saying: "Valuable to God is the death of his saints." If we will only get ourselves out of the way, then God could go ahead with His plans. This is one of the valuable outcomes of Paul's words in Galatians 2:20: "I am crucified with Christ: nevertheless I live; yet not I, but Christ liveth in me: and the life which I now live in the flesh I live by the faith of the Son of God, who loved me, and gave himself for me." Paul saw himself out of the way. He was alive, but the one in control was the indwelling Christ. That is why he said in Philippians 1:21: "For to me to live is Christ, and to die is gain."

Paul did not live to copy Christ, or to imitate Christ, or even to follow Christ. His whole life was a continuous involvement with the living Lord.

Verse 13 of our Psalm is speaking of the death of the Savior. Verse 15 is speaking of the death of the saint. This is one of the landmarks on the way to experiencing rest. Inasmuch as I am willing to die to self, in that much I am valuable to God and also, in that much, I begin to experience the rest for which I am longing.

I wrote the following words in my Bible the other day, for they seem to sum up what we have been thinking—"He died that I might live, now I must die, so that He can live."

Having established the need for getting ourselves out of the way, the next question is, "How can I make this real in my own life?" This is the message found in verse 17. This also is the third thing being taught in this psalm. Verse 15 tells of the need to die, verse 17 tells how this can be accomplished in the experience of the Christian.

Verse 16 underlines the relationship between us and God, reminding us of our true position and emphasizing our earnest devotion: "O Lord, truly I am thy servant: I am thy servant, and the son of thy handmaid: thou hast loosed my bonds."

Then come the motivating words of verse 17: "I will offer to thee the sacrifice of thanksgiving, and will call upon the name of the Lord." The culminating point in this search for rest is the offering to God of the sacrifice of thanksgiving. For the Christian this is spelled out in Romans 12:1: "I beseech you therefore, brethren, by the mercies of God, that ye present your bodies a living sacrifice, holy, acceptable unto God, which is your reasonable service."

These words are often referred to, often quoted, and often used, but what is needed now is an involvement in the act, a willingness to present our bodies as a living sacrifice. We need to realize this is a continuous and a continual process. There is the one act of presenting myself, but this must be followed by the activity of living in the sacrificial relationship. We need to watch out for the danger of only making "the act" of presenting ourselves, of coming with our hearts stirred and our minds willing in true sincerity. Then, having performed the act of yielding to the Lord, we imagine that the deed is accomplished and we have done what was required.

Verse 1 says: "Present your bodies a living sacrifice." See the special distinction?—it is to be a living sacrifice. This is most unusual. All the sacrifices offered in the Temple were dying sacrifices. The animal who was offered died, and that was the completion of the sacrifice. With us it is the opposite, the one who is offered lives and so the sacrifice is a continual yielding of our hearts and lives to God.

Notice also what it is we have to present — our bodies. The same thought is found in Romans 6:13: "Yield yourselves unto God, as those that are alive from the dead, and your members as instruments of righteousness unto God." Here there is the same idea of a living offering—"alive from the dead."

We have to yield our members as instruments of righteousness unto God. Our members means our bodies, our faculties, all that we have and are. We are to present them as "instruments" unto God. This word "instruments" means tools, weapons, or implements. This becomes a very demanding and a practical involvement.

As instructed by verse 15 in the Psalm, we see ourselves out of the way. We die to self so that we can be valuable to God. Then, with self as the dominating factor gone, we present to God the full use of our bodies and our faculties. We seek to allow the indwelling Christ to take control of all that we are and have. We do this day by day, and moment by moment. This is the meaning of the words: "For me to live is Christ . . . Christ is living in me."

Romans 12:2 tells us what will happen as a result of this presentation: "And be not conformed to this world: but be ye transformed by the renewing of your mind, that ye may prove what is that good, and acceptable, and perfect, will of God." As we learn to go on day by day, yielding each decision, each temptation, each problem and fear to the living Christ who indwells us, then we will begin to grow in grace. This will not be an instantaneous change, but a gradual growth.

I have known young people who have come to me several weeks after yielding their lives to Christ, complaining that they could see no change in their lives. They were wondering what had gone wrong. They were like the little boy who planted some seeds, then kept on digging them up to see if they were growing. The Bible promises that there will be a transformation, but notice how it is expressed: "Be not conformed to this world: but be ye transformed." God expects my co-operation in this whole process. Phillips' translation has a good word here: "Don't let the world around you squeeze you into its own mold, but let God remold your minds from within." If I deliberately go on putting myself in the places and situations where the world exerts its pressures on my life, then I must not be surprised if I am squeezed into the mold of a broken failing world. If I am not to be conformed to this world then it takes both faith and works—my faith and my works.

If I choose to commit myself moment by moment into the hands of Christ then He, the divine potter, will fashion me anew and my life will be transformed. Notice again there must be the act of yielding followed by the activity of yielding to Christ.

Verse 2 tells us also how and where this transformation takes place, "by the renewing of your mind." It starts on the inside and works its way out. It is not adhering to a set of outward rules, or conforming to a denominational or cultural pattern. It begins in the mind. Philippians 2:5 says: "Let this mind be in you, which was also in Christ Jesus." The only way you can have the mind of Christ is when Christ has the mind of you. And the only way this can become true in your experience is when you choose to yield to Him your mind, to present your body, to yield your members.

There is no easy, press-button way of experiencing real rest—peace of mind and rest of soul. You have to work at it, the work of faith. You have to realize the wonderful threefold offer of salvation that comes from "the Lord [who] hath dealt bountifully with thee." Then, finally you have to make the threefold response of taking the cup of salvation, of being prepared to see yourself dead to your own will, and of presenting your whole being a living sacrifice—with the accent on the living!

April 13th

8

God's Fireworks

Psalm 110

The Lord said unto my Lord, Sit thou at my right hand, until I make thine enemies thy footstool.

The Lord shall send the rod of thy strength out of Zion: rule thou in the midst of thine enemies.

Thy people shall be willing in the day of thy power, in the beauties of holiness from the womb of the morning: thou hast the dew of thy youth.

The Lord hath sworn, and will not repent, Thou art a priest for ever after the order of Melchizedek.

The Psalm is a perfect example of that which the Lord Jesus referred to when He said: "all things must be fulfilled, which were written in the law of Moses, and in the prophets, and in the psalms, concerning me" (Luke 24:44). There are vitally important things which have been fulfilled, there are equally important things which have yet to be fulfilled. And the point is that they should be, they could be, and they ought to be fulfilled in our lives now, day by day.

Look at verse 1 of this Psalm: "The Lord said unto my Lord, Sit thou at my right hand, until I make thine enemies thy footstool." The Lord Jesus referred to this in Mark 12:36. The interesting thing here is to see the authority He gave to the psalm: "For David himself said by the Holy Ghost, The Lord said to my Lord. . . ." Jesus said these words were written by the Holy Spirit through the medium of David. This prophecy has already been fulfilled. Jesus is already at the right hand of God, waiting to see His enemies become His footstool.

Now look at verse 4: "The Lord hath sworn, and will not repent, Thou art a priest for ever after the order of Melchizedek." This verse is mentioned in two places in Hebrews. In 5:6 we read: "As he saith also in another place, Thou art a priest for ever after the order of Melchisedec." Notice that God is said to be the originator of the words, although David penned them.

In 7:17 it says: "For he testifieth, Thou art a priest for ever after the order of Melchisedec." Once again God is the speaker. Again we can recognize that this prophecy has been fulfilled. Hebrews 8:1 says: "We have such an high priest, who is set on the right hand of the throne of the Majesty in the heavens."

Christ has successfully fulfilled all that was spoken of Him in this Psalm — but how about us in our response?

Look at Psalm 110:3: "Thy people shall be willing in the day of thy power." These words were written in the future tense, speaking of a group of people who would be "willing" in the day when Christ had received the power. If we look in Matthew 28:18 we can see some vital words spoken by Christ: "And Jesus came and spake unto them, saying, All power is given unto me in heaven and in earth." Notice who it is speaking—this is the risen victorious Christ, claiming that He has all the power. In the same context, the end of verse 20 records: "And, lo, I am with you alway, even unto the end of the world."

So the future time referred to in the Psalm has arrived. Jesus has the power, and He is with us each one, as He indwells us by His Holy Spirit. There is only one problem—His people are not willing. This is so obvious as I travel the world and see the state of the Church in many countries. There is plenty of talk and planning, many committees and organizations, but a striking absence of believers who are prepared to face up to the fact of a total surrender to Christ. So few are willing to be involved at all personal levels with the One who possesses all the power.

Because of this unwillingness to be involved with the risen indwelling Christ who has all the power, vast areas of unfinished work still exist across the world. The biggest area of need is in the hearts and lives of Christians. There are those who are barren and dry, whose lives know nothing of the fruitfulness that Christ expects and looks for. There are those who are defeated by sin and temptation, whose daily lives are a mere shadow of what they could be if they were willing to co-operate with the Lord. There are others who are bewildered by doubts and fears, anxiety and frustration, because they, too, have never been willing to get involved with the One who has all the power and all the answers to their needs.

Because there are such areas of need in the hearts of God's people, there are also great corresponding weaknesses in Christian service, in missions, in evangelism, in bringing the Gospel to all people in this our day and generation.

But, just as this Psalm reveals the need and the failure, it also indicates how the weakness can be put right. There is a beautiful thought tucked away in verse 2: "The Lord shall send the rod of thy strength out of Zion: rule thou in the midst of thine enemies."

When I was meditating the other day about the unwilling people and how the Lord was going to use a rod in deliverance, my mind went back to a fascinating story in the Old Testament. It was about a man who was very unwilling. It was also about his rod, and what happened when he became willing.

You will find the beginning of the story in Exodus 3. God had a tremendous plan prepared to redeem His people from the bondage of Egypt, and to take them into the fruitful land of Canaan. All the plans were ready, all the power was available, only one thing was missing—a man through whom God could bring His whole work to fruition.

God was ready, but the man was not. Moses, we know, was to be that man, but at the beginning of chapter 3 he is in the place of failure. For forty years Moses had enjoyed unique privileges in Egypt. Social status, education, training—everything had been his, but he had lost everything in a moment of self-will. Politically he had destroyed himself, and to save his own skin he had fled the country. Exodus 2:21 tells us that he who had enjoyed so much was "content" to dwell in the desert—he was content to be a failure. This was to be his daily experience for the next forty years. He spent forty years going upward, then the next forty years going down, until he was back where he started.

Exodus 3:1 tells us he was in the back side of the desert—an insignificant nobody, eighty years old, living in an insignificant place—and yet this was to be God's man, when God had dealt with him.

The chapter begins with the story of the burning bush: "And he looked, and, behold, the bush burned with fire, and the bush was not consumed." God was showing Moses a new quality of life he had never seen before. The bush was alive and growing, yet into the bush there came a living fire so that the bush became the vehicle for the fire—and yet the bush was not consumed. The bush was as insignificant as Moses was, one of many such ordinary desert plants. But when the fire got into the bush the whole situation was changed, new life was seen. It was this that caused Moses to say: "I will now turn aside, and see this great sight, why the bush is not burnt."

First, he looked, then he turned aside to see why.

It was when Moses turned aside to find out how and why such a miracle of new life came about, it was then that God spoke to him. God was using this vivid visual aid to show Moses a new principle of life, and Moses was quick enough to recognize the thing when he saw it—now he wanted to know how the principle worked. God was to go on to show Moses that what He could do with a bush — an insignificant, dry, dusty, desert bush, He could do with a man—an insignificant, dry, dusty, desert man. God's problem was to get the fire inside the man!

The wonder of this first encounter with God never left Moses. Even at the end of his life, forty years later, it was still vivid in his memory. In Deuteronomy 33:1 we read: "And this is the blessing, wherewith Moses the man of God blessed the children of Israel before his death." Then follows the record of the inspired words that came from his lips as he spoke concerning each tribe in turn. Verses 13-17 record the special blessing God had reserved for Joseph. Verse 16 says: "And for the precious things of the earth and fulness thereof, and for the good will of him that dwelt in the bush: let the blessing come upon the head of Joseph, and upon the top of the head of him that was separated from his brethren."

The greatest blessing sought for Joseph's descendants was that which happened to Moses—and to Joseph. For Joseph was separated as Moses was. Moses was in a desert, Joseph in a dungeon, but the fire of God got into the heart of Joseph, and Joseph, the despised and the rejected, became God's man at the beginning of the years in Egypt just as Moses became God's man at the end. And the secret in each case was, "the good will of him that dwelt in the bush." That same good will dwelt in Moses throughout the forty years in the wilderness. He never forgot it, it was his basis for living—because God got the fire inside the man.

There is a challenging message for us in all this. We may not be in the desert, or in the dungeon, but we can be God's men and women for our day and generation. Acts 2:1-4 tells a similar story about another group of insignificant men and women. They were gathered with a sense of insecurity and uncertainty when:

> *suddenly there came a sound from heaven as of a rushing mighty wind, and it filled all the house where they were sitting.*
>
> *And there appeared unto them cloven tongues like as of fire, and it sat upon each of them.*
>
> *And they were all filled with the Holy Ghost.*

The fire that sat on them, got inside them and they became the vehicles for the Lord. They burned, but were not consumed. The new quality of life was seen in them, as they were filled with the Spirit. And once again God began to lead captives out of the bondage of their own sins into the Canaan of his grace. Once again the good will of Him that dwelt in the bush was operating through a host of insignificant "bushes."

We who believe and call ourselves Christians are in that same company today. We are the bushes of God, but no one will turn aside to see—because the bushes are not burning. If we are believers then we possess the same Holy Spirit. In one sense the fire is in us, all the potential is there. There is only one problem—the bushes do not burn. This is so obvious when we see the absence of what should follow "a burning bush" experience. Fire has the capacity to do many amazing things. One of the greatest of these is to purify everything with which it comes in contact—whatever remains after the fire has burned, is pure and free from all disease and impurity.

I remember, when we were in Australia, in the Brisbane area, we saw fire being used to help in harvesting the sugar cane crop. There were vast fields of towering sugar cane over eight and ten feet tall. Each cane had reached sugar perfection within. Each cane was covered with dead dry leaves coming out of the tall stem all the way up. In these dead leaves many bugs and insects were living—a source of potential danger in the days ahead. When the crop was ready, the farmer chose a day when the wind was in the right direction and blowing at the right speed. Fire was applied to the tall canes on the windward side of the field and soon the field became an inferno as the flames swept across the whole area. As we watched, it looked as if everything was being destroyed. Towering clouds of smoke arose, lit up by the flames below, until the fire had finished its work.

When we saw the finished product we saw the wisdom of purifying by fire. All the dead brown leaves had vanished. All the insects and areas of disease had been destroyed. All that was left were the tall canes full of sweetness.

If the fire burned in "the bushes of God" all the old dead leaves would vanish, all the bugs and areas of spiritual disease would be swept away by the Spirit's purifying power. But when fire does not burn, then the dead leaves accumulate and provide homes for potential carriers of disease.

Fire not only purifies, it also protects. In Moses' day, and in our day also, a good fire blazing at night can be used to keep away dangerous animals from any who are camping out, or living in the open spaces. It is just the same in Christian experience. If the fire is burning in our hearts and lives, many of the experiences and attacks of the enemy will be thwarted by the Spirit's protective fire.

Everything depends upon getting the fire inside, and keeping the fire burning. Let the Spirit bless our hearts as we turn once more to the story of Moses in Exodus 3 and find how God got the fire in His chosen man.

First, Moses looked, then he turned aside to see—then God spoke. God will always speak to anyone who will turn aside to see. God's first lesson for Moses was the fact of holiness. Moses began by recognizing the holiness of God. It was a lesson he never forgot all his life—a burning bush is always a holy bush! Then God went on to outline the background to the whole situation of the children of Israel. He spoke of their sufferings and of His plans to "bring them up out of that land unto a good land and a large, unto a land flowing with milk and honey" (verse 8).

In verse 10 God gave His first invitation to Moses: "Come now therefore, and I will send thee unto Pharaoh, that thou mayest bring forth my people the children of Israel out of Egypt." Moses' immediate reaction was to find excuses for not being involved. In verse 11 he said: "Who am I," pleading his insignificance. To which God replied, "Certainly I will be with thee." Moses countered this by asking "Who are you" —"when they shall say to me, What is his name? what shall I say unto them?" (verse 13).

The Lord then went on to give a glorious account of exactly what He was planning to do. He supplied interesting details to whet the interest and appetite of Moses. Moses listened to all this in silence, and then, when God had finished speaking he replied in 4:1 with a miserably unenthusiastic "But. . . ." Moses was obsessed with the idea of his uselessness, and his unsuitability. After all he was over eighty years old, and his last forty years had been empty years of failure—caring for a flock of sheep and goats was hardly a suitable preparation, in the eyes of Moses, for such a testing time of adventure and action.

It was then that the Lord came to grips with this personal problem in the life of Moses. Exodus 4:2 says: "And the Lord said unto him, What is that in thine hand? And he said, A rod." God took him up on his own ground and focused the attention on his rod. This rod was his shepherd's staff. It was, in a way, a symbol of his failure. The same hand had held a sword in his previous experience in Egypt—the symbol of his own self will—wherewith he had slain the Egyptian. The same hand had held the rod of power when he was a prince, the son of Pharaoh's daughter.

This hand had known many exciting experiences, but now all was lost, and all he had was a rod, a simple, common, everyday shepherd's rod.

The Lord then told him to cast it down—a test of simple obedience. When Moses did so he got the shock of his life. This simple rod, this useless thing, was suddenly changed into a serpent. Previously Moses had been clinging to his rod as his one excuse for avoiding involvement with God. Now he fled from it—his excuse was gone, it had turned into an enemy.

The Lord then told Moses to do something absolutely stupid: "Put forth thine hand, and take it by the tail." What a crazy thing to do. Moses' forty years of desert experience had long since taught him never to take a serpent by its tail—always grasp it behind the head. If he took it by the tail, it would lash around and bite him. But once again he obeyed the Lord and this time the impossible happened—the serpent became a rod once more. The rod, which had previously been his excuse for non-involvement, now took on a totally new significance. If God could do such things with an ordinary, worthless rod, what could He do with an insignificant, worthless man?

So it is we find that the rod which had been the symbol of his failure, gradually became the sign of his faith. The succeeding verses in chapter 4 go on to tell how God dealt yet more with this man. Little by little his unwillingness began to disappear until it became obvious that Moses was going to commit himself—just as he was—to the hands of the great God who was speaking with him.

Just before he moved away from the burning bush to step into a new life the Lord said these words to him: "And thou shalt take this rod in thine hand, wherewith thou shalt do signs" (verse 17). The key to the whole situation was the rod. In fact, the words of verse 20 take on a new significance: "And Moses took his wife and his sons . . . and he returned to the land of Egypt: and Moses took the rod of God in his hand." At the beginning of the interview it was the rod of Moses, at the end it was the rod of God. It was the same rod in each case, but there had been a change of ownership. The glory of it all was that God did not only own the rod—He also owned the man and the rod.

The fire had got inside of Moses, and he who had been an insignificant failure became the man through whom God was going to do great and mighty exploits. The fire was never extinguished. It purified Moses, it protected Moses, it empowered him. Such was his life that, at the very end, in Deuteronomy 34:7 we read: "And Moses was an hundred and twenty years old when he died: his eye was not dim, nor his natural force abated." Verse 10 adds: "And there arose not a prophet since in Israel like unto Moses, whom the Lord knew face to face." The face to face existence began at the burning bush and it ended when God buried him "in a valley in the land of Moab . . . but no man knoweth of his sepulchre unto this day" (verse 6).

The message in all this for us is so plain to see. What excuse do you have for not being willing in this the day of His power? What kind of a rod do you hold in your hand? Is it something insignificant in your eyes, just as it was with Moses? Is your rod the symbol of your failure? Why not turn aside and see? Let God speak to you. Hear Him tell you to cast down your excuse, your weakness, your failure. Then see it for what it is, a serpent, a sinful thing that is keeping you from God's will for your life. Let your rod become God's "rod," then, once more the fire will begin to burn. As you expose to its purifying flames all the deadness and disease in your heart you, too, will know a cleansing that will prepare you to become the vehicle for the life of Christ.

The same fire of the indwelling Christ will protect you and guard you, just as we read in First John 4:4: "Ye are of God, little children, and have overcome them: because greater is he that is in you, than he that is in the world."

In all this the truth of Psalm 110:3 will be seen in your life: "Thy people shall be willing in the day of thy power, in the beauties of holiness from the womb of the morning: thou hast the dew of thy youth." The holiness that characterized Moses will be seen in you, and you, too, will know a new sense of life as "the dew of thy youth" is shed abroad in your heart through the indwelling Christ.

9

Jesus and the Rebels

Psalm 68

Once again, as we turn to this Psalm, we see those distinguishing features which mark it off as one of those special Psalms in which we find the risen, victorious Christ.

This is especially so in verse 18 where we read: "Thou hast ascended on high, thou hast led captivity captive: thou hast received gifts for men." These words are cited in Ephesians 4:8: "Wherefore he saith, When he ascended on high, he led captivity captive, and gave gifts unto men."

The interesting thing in this Psalm is to see to whom those gifts are specially designated. Verse 18 continues: "Yea, for the rebellious also, that the Lord God might dwell among them."

At the beginning of the Psalm we read of the goodness of the Lord to certain groups of people. Verses 5 and 6 say: "A father of the fatherless, and a judge of the widows, is God in his holy habitation.

"God setteth the solitary in families: he bringeth out those which are bound with chains." These are the loving acts of a gracious heavenly Father. But then there comes a word of condemnation: "But the rebellious dwell in a dry land." God had blessing for everyone, but the rebels were excluded to a dry land.

This is the situation, the exclusion of all rebels, until we come to the verse we have already mentioned. In other words, the resurrection of Christ changed things for everyone.

This is the importance of verse 18: "Thou hast received gifts for men"—then comes the special emphasis—"yea, for the rebellious also." For the first time there is a new opportunity for rebels. Notice what that opportunity is: "That the Lord God might dwell among them." Previously they had been in a dry place, segregated to loneliness and deadness; now they can come and receive gifts from the risen Christ so that God may dwell among them.

I find these words have taken on a new meaning over these last few years. There was a time when rebellion was a thing confined to the non-Christian and to such as were anti-God in their outlook. But the increased freedom of thought, based often on little knowledge and more prejudice, has given rise to areas of rebellion in the hearts of many Christians, old and young.

In many cases there were genuine grounds for their feelings of unrest and dissatisfaction. Things did need to be revised and altered. The tragedy was that what started out as a reason somehow became changed to a rebellion.

This is sad because, as the Psalm so wisely puts it, "the rebellious dwell in a dry land." Many of those who were swayed into rebellion came to find themselves dwelling in a desert of discontent. This is true not only of spiritual values but in every walk of life. There are many campus rebels who were once eloquent in their denunciations, but who are now living in deserts of uselessness and areas of aridness.

This then is the beauty and the wonder of this Psalm. There *is* an answer to the dead dryness of rebellion with all its negative associations—that answer is in the risen Christ.

Look now in Ephesians 4:11-13 as it is seen in the Amplified Version:

> *And His gifts were [varied; He Himself appointed and gave men to us,] some to be apostles (special messengers), some prophets (inspired preachers and expounders), some evangelists (preachers of the Gospel, traveling missionaries), some pastors (shepherds of His flock) and teachers.*
>
> *His intention was the perfecting* and *the full equipping of the saints (His consecrated people),* [*that they should do*] *the work of ministering toward building up Christ's body (the church),*
>
> [*That it might develop*] *until we all attain oneness in the faith and in the comprehension of the full and accurate knowledge of the Son of God; that* [*we might arrive*] *at really mature manhood —the completeness of personality which is nothing less than the standard height of Christ's own perfection—the measure of the stature of the fullness of the Christ,* and *the completeness found in Him.*

These are wonderful words, tremendous in their implications and so life-changing in their application. Jesus gave gifts to men so that all might come to really mature manhood, to a completeness of personality.

There may be someone reading this to whom these words can come with new life-saving power. You, too, may be a rebel, young or old. Your reasons for your rebellion may be varied—selfish, idealistic, enthusiastic. Maybe you have never looked upon yourself as a real rebel but just as an honest grumbler or complainer. You may have good reasons for your feelings, but you cannot alter the fact that "the rebellious dwell in a dry place."

It is to you, especially, that the risen Christ gives a new opportunity to grow on to really mature manhood, with a new sense of completeness of personality.

How does He bring this about in your experience? By your coming to a full and accurate knowledge of the Son of God. Ignorance is often the root cause of much of our rebellion against the Lord. We have never fully understood who Jesus Christ is and what He has come to do in our hearts. We have half the facts, and we proceed to make a judgment on the little knowledge we possess.

Every true believer knows the value and the wonder of the death of Christ. It is through this precious death that we are born again. Through His sacrifice we have forgiveness of our sins and the full assurance of a home in heaven. This is wonderful, but this is not all there is for us in Christ. Verse 13 speaks of knowing the fullness of Christ, and the completeness found in Him. This is a reference to what the Bible calls the saving life of Christ. The work of Christ on the cross is the finished work of Christ associated with His saving death. But then the Bible speaks of the unfolding work of Christ as He indwells us by His Holy Spirit. Every believer is indwelt by the risen Christ, but not every believer is filled by the risen Christ. Verse 13 speaks of knowing the fullness of Christ.

Every believer is indwelt by the Holy Spirit, but not every such believer is filled with the Holy Spirit. Remember that being filled with the Holy Spirit is the same as being filled with the fullness of Christ because Jesus indwells me by His Holy Spirit. The Holy Spirit's work is to make Jesus real in my life.

This is what it means in the Psalm, verse 18, when it says: "Gifts for men; yea, for the rebellious also, that the Lord God might dwell among them." The Psalm says the gifts even for the rebellious were that God might dwell among them. The corresponding words in Ephesians 4:13 are "that Christ may dwell in you."

God's answer to the rebel is to reveal to him the fullness of Christ—to show that he is not just a solitary person battling against the injustices of life, struggling to change the world through his own willing sacrifice. God loves to show us His complete plan which can come true in our lives only when we are complete in Christ. If I want to experience life and real purpose in living, then I must recognize the indwelling Christ, let Him take control of my life and let Him use me in His great plan for world revolution. Jesus Christ does not want rebels, but partners in His own plan to bring about a new world. He is busy making new people here on earth. Some day He will make a new heaven and a new earth in which these new people will live. This is real revolution. There is nothing dry or disappointing in His great plan.

But then this idea of having the fullness of Christ is not just a theological expression, it leads on to practical realities. I am assured by God's Word that if I have a new life in Christ, then I will have a new "walk" in the world.

There are many honest rebels whose one desire is to change the world, to make the world a better place in which to live. The Bible teaches that the way to change the world is, first of all, to bring about a radical change in one's own life. It tells me how this can be done. It teaches a technique which has stood the test of time. God is not dependent on the changing philosophies of men, for His way is perfect. His plan has been tested and tried down through the ages and has been responsible for much of the improvement in social and economic conditions throughout the earth. God's plan is to use changed men to change the world. Changing men is God's prerogative—only He can do this. Second Corinthians 5:17 says: "Therefore if any man be in Christ, he is a new creature." God's way is to put the man in Christ and to put Christ in the man. This is what the Psalm is saying in verse 18, and this is what Ephesians 4:13 is promising—a new sense of completeness found only in Christ.

When the rebel has that completeness of personality, that mature manhood, then he can demonstrate to the world a new walk. In this way the world sees a changed man or a changed woman. The trouble with so many of us is that we are idealistic in thinking and speaking, and just plain old failures when it comes to living. The world around us never sees our changed walk—it only hears our changed talk.

This is why the Holy Spirit in Ephesians 4:17-19 says:

> *This I say therefore, and testify in the Lord, that ye henceforth walk not as other Gentiles walk, in the vanity of their mind.*
>
> *Having the understanding darkened, being alienated from the life of God through the ignorance that is in them, because of the blindness of their heart:*
>
> *Who being past feeling have given themselves over to lasciviousness, to work all uncleanness with greediness.*

This is the way we used to walk, in the blindness of our own hearts. Then verses 20 and 21 come with the tremendous challenge: "But ye have not so learned Christ, If so be that ye have heard him, and have been taught by him, as the truth is in Jesus." That is the testing-point—have we learned Christ, as the truth is in Jesus? This has nothing to do with religion or ritual—this is reality, Christ, the truth in Jesus. If the truth is in Jesus and Jesus is in me, then the truth is in me, in Jesus.

That is why the rest of Ephesians 4 goes on to a detailed description of the changed walk of the changed man. This is not rebellion, it is revolution demonstrated through really mature manhood.

There are seven characteristics of this new walk. Let us see them as we go on through the verses 22-32. First, verse 22 tells us to put off the old way of life. It likens this old way to an old dirty, stained and ragged garment. It shows the stains and smells of old associations. We have to strip it off and discard it altogether.

Then verse 23 brings in the thought of a *new mind.* It says: "And be renewed in the spirit of your mind." This is where the change begins. Philippians 2:5 says: "Let this mind be in you, which was also in Christ Jesus." Because I have the presence of Christ, I have the mind of Christ. As I yield to Him in my mind so that His will is being done, then my mind is renewed. Some people concentrate on improving their habits and other external evidences—this is the wrong order. The first essential in the new walk is to have a new mind.

Verse 24 goes on to speak of the *new man*: "And that ye put on the new man, which after God is created in righteousness and true holiness." If the new mind is in control, then the new man will be seen. If the old man is still trying to improve the situation then the old man will still be seen. Notice that this is a work of faith. We do not wait for God to strip us of the old, and then to help us into our new life—as a mother helping a little child. We are to strip ourselves and then to put on the new man. God seeks my willing co-operation.

Because there is a new man in control, and a new mind planning and directing, several practical results will be seen in our daily lives. Verse 25 speaks of a *new member*: "Wherefore putting away lying, speak every man truth with his neighbour: for we are members one of another." The picture here is of a body with its many parts—members means the parts of the body. We are to see ourselves as parts of a body. First Corinthians 12:12 says: "For as the body is one, and hath many members, and all the members of that one body, being many, are one body: so also is Christ." Verse 27 adds: "Now ye are the body of Christ, and members in particular." The normal human body is well-coordinated. As it walks down the street, every member plays its part in the physical act of walking. The body walks as a unit. Lack of coordination produces the walk of the physically handicapped or the spastic.

Thus, the first outcome seen from the new man with the new mind, is a unity with my brothers and sisters in Christ—marked by new truth and honesty. I find there is a lot of talk these days about the Church and the need for an increased ecumenical involvement. The Bible uses the picture of "the Body of Christ" as the concept of all true believers. My human life is in every part of my body. In just the same way the life of Christ is in every part of the body of Christ. All the members share the "Life" in actuality. There is no need for a body to strive for ecumenicity. It already has a oneness. The body of Christ has no artificial limbs!

As if to stress this need for control in the body of Christ the next verses in Ephesians 4, 26 and 27, tell of a *new master*: "Be ye angry, and sin not: let not the sun go down upon your wrath; Neither give place to the devil."

These words show us plainly that the Christian is not necessarily a colorless, cold specimen. It speaks of an anger which is not a sin. The Lord Jesus on several occasions was moved to show strong emotional feelings, but always without sin. The whole emphasis here is on control — not self-control, but control by the new Master, the risen, victorious indwelling Christ. As I recognize Him as my Lord and my Savior, then I will not give place to the devil. When Christ fills my life there is no room for the devil. It is good, here, to point out that being filled with Christ does not mean my having more of Christ—as if He came in different proportions. It means Christ having more of me. As I open the doors to the various areas in my life then He has more of me. If I only allow Him a couple of hours on Sunday, plus panic time when I am in serious trouble, then He will not fill much of my life. There will be space enough to give place to the devil — and this is what often happens.

As I grow in the faith and the Lord reveals to me new areas for Him to control, then it is my responsibility to yield to Him as He shows me. This is called growing in grace. This is how young children at an early age can come and trust Christ as their own Savior. They do so within the context of their limited knowledge of themselves and of Him, and of life around. But, as they grow on to be juniors then seniors, they become aware of new areas in their personality. Their task is to keep on yielding as He keeps on revealing. In this way they increase in the fullness of Christ, and in this way they keep on giving no place to the devil.

The tragedy is when those who become Christians at an early age allow that measure of the fullness of Christ to remain static through their growing years. To have a six-year-old's sense of the fullness of Christ when you are sixteen years old is asking for trouble. You have grown a lot in ten years, not only physically, but in personality and emotional ability. If Jesus is only controlling, as it were, a six-year-old area in a sixteen-year-old life—then there will be plenty of space for the devil. Be assured he knows how to make good use of it—or bad use of it!

Verse 28 comes with a rugged, practical challenge as it speaks of a *new method:* "Let him that stole steal no more: but rather let him labor, working with his hands the thing which is good, that he may have to give to him that needeth." This is showing that the new method in the new life is to be in complete contrast to the old way of life. If a man stole from people, then he had to give to people—and what he gave he had to earn by his own hands. This opens up a good principle for us to follow. What was your area of weakness as a non-Christian becomes the basis of contrast in your new life. If you were a proud person, Christ will make you a gracious humble person. If you were soon angry then Christ will change you to a loving, kindly person.

This is what He did to John, the beloved disciple. We read in Mark 3:13-19 how the Lord Jesus ordained the twelve to be with Him. Verse 17 says: "And James the son of Zebedee, and John the brother of James; and he surnamed them Boanerges, which is,

The sons of thunder." A fuller meaning for Boanerges is "the soon angry ones." This was how Christ found John when He first met him — quick-tempered, soon angry. But when we meet John in his epistles we see the direct opposite. The work of Chirst in the heart and life of John had changed him from the braggart to the beloved.

This is what should happen in every Christian life when the new Master by His new mind brings a new method in our yielded lives.

Ephesians 4:29, 30 go on to amplify this thought of the new method. When the new method becomes established in the life of the believer, then we see a *new ministry* emerging: "Let no corrupt communication proceed out of your mouth, but that which is good to the use of edifying, that it may minister grace unto the hearers.

"And grieve not the Spirit of God, whereby ye are sealed unto the day of redemption."

Having dealt with the new mind in verse 23 the results are now seen through the new mouth. God works from the inside to the outside. He changes the man on the inside, then the world sees the change on the outside. This is the same plan we saw earlier in this chapter — using changed men to change the world. Words are important, very important. What I say or write may be negative, positive or neutral. It is only when I see the potential of the Christ indwelling me, and I allow Him by His Holy Spirit to take my lips and use them — it is only then that there comes a Christ-centered positive message through my lips.

Notice also that grieving the Holy Spirit is linked with the words that come from my mouth. Not only what I do, but especially what I say can cause grief to the blessed Spirit of God.

The seventh characteristic of the new walk listed in this chapter is found in the last two verses. This is simple Christian living day by day—a demonstration of *new manners:* "Let all bitterness, and wrath, and anger, and clamour, and evil speaking, be put away from you, with all malice:

"And be ye kind one to another, tenderhearted, forgiving one another, even as God for Christ's sake hath forgiven you."

These words are an amplification of the new ministry and the new method mentioned above. Here are the opposites and the contrasts. It is good to see that the theological teaching of the chapter ends up not on the bookshelf but in the kitchen—right where the action is. All the things we want, the love, the kindness, the forgiveness—these are the finished product of a new walk with Christ. These outside enjoyments come because of an inside involvement—and there is no other way.

This then is what the Lord Jesus has for rebels—changed lives by which He can change the world. Any takers?

10

The Cross and the Christ

Psalm 22

Every Psalm has it own unique quality. This precious Psalm can be compared to going into the Holy of Holies in the Temple or the Tabernacle. In the days of the Old Testament the high priest was the only man who had the right of entrance, and he could step inside only on one day in the year—the day of Atonement. He went in with awe and wonder, with fear and trembling, because he was meeting a holy God. He took with him blood which he sprinkled on the mercy seat—in the presence of a holy God. The blood he carried was his only reason for going through the veil, it was his only protection and his hope.

Every other day in the year the veil hung between the priests and the mercy seat. The way into the Holiest was still closed and restricted. Thus it was for hundreds of years — until the day Jesus died on Calvary. Then Matthew gives us these words in 27:50, 51: "Jesus, when he had cried again with a loud voice, yielded up the ghost. And, behold, the veil of the temple was rent in twain from the top to the bottom . . . . " Notice from where the rending began—from the top. God split the veil right down the center—the way in was closed no longer!

This is why we read in Hebrews 10:19-22:

Having therefore, brethren, boldness to enter into the holiest by the blood of Jesus,

By a new and living way, which he hath consecrated for us, through the veil, that is to say, his flesh;

And having an high priest over the house of God;

Let us draw near with a true heart in full assurance of faith, having our hearts sprinkled from an evil conscience, and our bodies washed with pure water.

This is exactly what we do when we turn our attention to these holy words in Psalm 22. We draw near with true hearts, in full assurance of faith.

In each study in this book we have looked for Jesus—to see Jesus in the Psalms, especially to see the risen Christ, and the things yet to be fulfilled. We have seen things which could be fulfilled in our hearts and lives—even today. We will see our Lord once more in these wondrous words.

As we look at the scene unfolding before our eyes we see, first, the dying Savior, then, in a blessed way, we will see the risen Savior. It is this living Christ who is our special hope and joy today.

In the order of Jewish family life it was the mother's task to teach her children to say the Psalms. Every Jewish child would stand by the mother's knee and learn to repeat the heritage of worship, truth and poetry contained in these songs. I sometimes imagine a little boy called Jesus standing by His mother's knee. She would teach Him to say the Psalms. His little lips would say, with loving hope: "The Lord is my shepherd, I shall not want." I wonder what He thought when He learned Psalm 22 with all its sorrow and agony. Many times He would say: "My God, my God, why hast thou forsaken me?" What cold lonely words they would sound to a boy.

And yet there came a day, as recorded by Matthew in 27:46, "And about the ninth hour Jesus cried with a loud voice, Eli, Eli, lama sabachthani? that is to say, My God, my God, why hast thou forsaken me?"

This Psalm is full of prophecy which came true, even down to the details of words and actions. It begins, as we see, with the very words that came from the parched lips of the dying Christ, piercing through the midday darkness. You will notice that there was no answer to His question—nothing but the silence of a darkened heaven. Have you ever wondered why no one answered? If your only son was dying, and he cried out for your presence, would you remain indifferent if it was within your power to go to his side? But this is what God did—He left Him to die alone—for you and for me. The answer to the lonely question is seen in verse 3 of this same Psalm: "But thou art holy, O thou that inhabitest the praises of Israel." God was a holy God—God is ever a holy God, and as such He can have no dealing with sin.

Previous to Calvary Jesus was the holy, spotless, Lamb of God, pure and sinless. But Isaiah 53:4-6 tells us the truth:

> *Surely he hath borne our griefs, and carried our sorrows . . . But he was wounded for our transgressions, he was bruised for our iniquities: the chastisement of our peace was upon him . . . All we like sheep have gone astray; we have turned every one to his own way; and the Lord hath laid on him the iniquity of us all.*

There it is, "The Lord hath laid on him the iniquity of us all." Jesus bore His cross, and on that cross He bore our sin. Not even the cry of the dying Son could change the holiness of God. Thus it was and thus it ever will be. Consider now the hopeless attitude of men, still in their sins, who hope to be accepted by a holy God because of the lives they live, or the gifts they give, or the church office which they hold. They expect a holy God who forsook His own Son to change His attitude to receive them. What pathetic arrogance!

Not only are the words of the dying Christ foretold in this Psalm, but we can read also the words of His cruel enemies. If we check verse 8 with Matthew 27:43 we see the words of the chief priests and the scribes and elders: "He trusted in God; let him deliver him now, if he will have him: for he said, I am the Son of God."

Verses 14-18 in the Psalm are a miraculous foretelling of detailed events. We have here a detailed and vivid account of the act of crucifixion written, through David, by the Holy Spirit over three hundred years ago. The Romans were responsible for perfecting the torturous death of crucifixion, yet when David wrote these words the Roman Empire had not even begun! The Jewish method of execution was stoning. This can be seen in the Old Testament, in people such as Achan in Joshua 7:25, and in the New Testament with Stephen in Acts 7:58.

The whole purpose of crucifixion was to make the victim suffer as much pain as possible for as long a time as possible. Tens of thousands of wretched sufferers died inch by inch and minute by minute throughout the years of Roman rule.

Crucifixion began with the victim being flogged, so that his body was already cut and bleeding and quivering with pain. Then the man carried his cross, dragging it in a trail of blood to the site of his coming death. A deep hole had already been dug in the ground, into which the cross would eventually be lowered.

Arriving at the place of execution the cross was placed flat on the ground. The tough brutal soldiers then forced the victim to lie on the cross. There must have been some terrible struggles before this was done, in most cases. But Isaiah 53:7 tells us the reaction of Jesus: "He was oppressed, and he was afflicted, yet he opened not his mouth: he is brought as a lamb to the slaughter, and as a sheep before her shearers is dumb, so he openeth not his mouth." Jesus' only words were: "Father, forgive them; for they know not what they do" (Luke 23:34).

As the victim struggled and fought, the soldiers would stretch out one hand, as far as it would reach, then drive a spike through the palm, fixing the squirming fingers to their final resting place. The other hand was similarly nailed in place, again stretched as far as it would go. The feet were often crossed, and they, too, were nailed to the cross.

Then the soldiers raised the cross, and dropped it into the hole already prepared. This was part of the science of suffering. As the cross hit the bottom of the hole, the man's body continued its downward plunge, but the hands held fast and in doing so the joints of the body were pulled out of position. This was the ultimate in agony. They left the victim there to die from heat, cold, hunger, thirst, pain and the many contributory causes that would multiply to drag him down to his death. History records that a strong, tough man would take several days to die!

This is what Jesus bore for us. The cross was not a golden jewel to wear, or a sacred emblem to worship, it was a rough, wooden monster on which a man dragged out his life in agony. No wonder the hymn writer said:

When I survey the wondrous cross,
On which the Prince of glory died,
My richest gain I count but loss,
And pour contempt on all my pride.

Consider how the verses of the Psalm describe what we have just seen. Verses 14 and 15 use a most graphic way to describe the downward plunge of the body (and the subsequent build-up of hopeless agony and physical collapse): "I am poured out like water, and all my bones are out of joint: my heart is like wax; it is melted in the midst of my bowels.

"My strength is dried up like a potsherd; and my tongue cleaveth to my jaws; and thou hast brought me into the dust of death."

In the gospel accounts of the death of Christ there are several direct references to this Psalm. Both Matthew 27:35 and John 19:23 give a direct reference to the act of crucifixion as told in verse 16 of the Psalm: "They pierced my hands and my feet."

Verse 17 in the Psalm refers to the act of stripping all the clothing from the victim. The greatest shame in Jewish culture was to be naked: "I may tell all my bones: they look *and* stare upon me."

Verse 18 says: "They part my garments among them, and cast lots upon my vesture." These few simple words form the basis of an accurately fulfilled prophecy. John 19:23, 24 records: "Then the soldiers, when they had crucified Jesus, took his garments, and made four parts, to every soldier a part." This was the usual practice at every such occasion. All that the victim possessed, usually the rags he was wearing, became the perquisites of the quarternion of soldiers—the four men in the execution squad. The armor of a Roman soldier required much cleaning to keep it bright and shining. Cleaning rags were always in great demand. So it was they tore up and divided the garments of the Son of God. But then we read: "And also his coat: now the coat was without seam, woven from the top throughout."

I like to think that my Lord wore good clothes when He was here on earth. The New Testament has several references to the women who followed Him and who ministered to Him out of their substance. Luke 8:3 records: "And Joanna the wife of Chuza Herod's steward, and Susanna, and many others, which ministered unto him of their substance." These were people whose lives had been touched by the wondrous grace of Christ and, who, in return, bought for Him the necessities of life. Obviously one of the things so provided was His robe. As reported in the verse above, it was a specially good garment. It was without a seam. Our garments are usually made of several pieces of material cut to shape and stitched together, but the robe that Jesus wore was woven in one piece from the top, where it was narrow, to the bottom—a beautiful, high-class, expensive garment.

So it was, when the soldiers had torn up the other undergarments, they came to His robe. "They said therefore among themselves, Let us not rend it, but cast lots for it, whose it shall be." Roman soldiers were always inveterate gamblers, ready to try their "luck" any time. They carried dice which they loved to roll. Not far from my home in England is the Roman Wall which was built to keep back enemies from the north. Remains of Roman camps can still be seen and the ruts in the stones worn by the chariot wheels at the entrance of the gates. It is also possible to see a rectangle of squares cut in the stone where the soldiers gambled in their games of chance. So, at the foot of the cross, while the Son of God was paying the price of sin, these four soldiers rolled their dice—and one man won the robe.

In doing so, he and they fulfilled to the letter the prophecy of verse 18 in the Psalm.

All that we have considered so far in the Psalm, plus the other connecting verses, have a direct reference to the death of Christ. But there is one special verse that belongs to the same context, yet has a new and a gloriously triumphant message for our hearts.

In verse 22 the same Person is still speaking, and we read these words: "I will declare thy name unto my brethren: in the midst of the congregation will I praise thee." This verse presents a different thought in every way. This is a reference to what would yet come to pass: "I will declare thy name unto my brethren." It is this verse which has come as a great blessing to my heart.

I was meditating on these words some time ago, and they seemed to have a familiar ring as I said them aloud: "I will declare thy name unto my brethren." Then I recalled the words of Jesus in the Lord's prayer in John 17. This chapter is also an experience in the Holy of Holies as we read these blessed words: "These words spake Jesus, and lifted up his eyes to heaven, and said, Father, the hour is come; glorify thy Son, that thy Son also may glorify thee." Great and wonderful words were spoken such as these: "This is life eternal, that they might know thee the only true God, and Jesus Christ, whom thou hast sent."

In verses 6-19 Jesus prayed especially for His disciples. In verse 9 we read: "I pray for them: I pray not for the world, but for them which thou hast given me; for they are thine."

Then from verse 20 to the end, the Lord prayed for us: "Neither pray I for these alone, but for them also which shall believe on me through their word." Make sure you know and fully realize that the Lord Jesus prayed for you personally—this has been a great comfort to my soul! He went on in verse 21: "That they all may be one; as thou, Father, art in me, and I in thee, that they also may be one in us . . . that they may be one, even as we are one; I in them, and thou in me."

Then comes the last verse of the prayer, which is the glorious fulfillment of verse 22 in the Psalm. The Psalm said: "I will declare thy name unto my brethren." The prayer ends with these words: "I have declared unto them thy name, and will declare it." This is tremendous, but the real ultimate in joy is to see why Jesus had declared the name of the Father: "that the love wherewith thou hast loved me may be in them, and I in them." There it is—"I in them." In Psalm 22, the first twenty-one verses are speaking of the death of Christ, all that He did when He died *for* us on the cross. They are telling of the saving death of Christ.

The twenty-second verse is telling the wonder of Jesus *in* us, the saving life of Christ, all that He can be to us day by day, as He dwells in our hearts and lives. Because He dwells in me, then the love of God can fill my heart and the power of Christ can fill my life. This is one of those jewels to which Christ was referring when He said: "You will find me in the Psalms."

Have you found Him— the living, victorious Christ— real in your heart day by day? This is why He died, this is why He rose again, this is why He prayed in John 17—that you might know love and peace, power and joy.

Remember, Jesus prayed for you — and He prayed that this experience might be yours — day by day!

11

The Pierced Ear

Psalm 40

This Psalm is a simple unfolding of truth. It tells us first the results of the love of God in our own experience. Then it details, in a unique way, the cost of that love, and how Jesus paid it for us. All this then becomes a challenge to our own hearts, that we should respond in a like manner to Him who first loved us.

The first five verses list for us, in beautiful language, what God has done. This is how David described it with regard to his own experience. Compare and see how true this is for you:

> *I waited patiently for the Lord; and he inclined unto me, and heard my cry.*
>
> *He brought me up also out of an horrible pit, out of the miry clay, and set my feet upon a rock, and established my goings.*
>
> *And he hath put a new song in my mouth, even praise unto our God: many shall see it, and fear, and shall trust in the Lord.*
>
> *Blessed is that man that maketh the Lord his trust, and respecteth not the proud, nor such as turn aside unto lies.*
>
> *Many, O Lord my God, are thy wonderful works which thou hast done, and thy thoughts which are to us-ward: they cannot be reckoned*

up in order unto thee: if I would declare and speak of them, they are more than can be numbered.

Notice the personal relationship in all these words. "I" was the one who waited patiently, and "He" was the one who did all the rest. There is a lesson for us here. Perhaps some reading these words feel that this has not come true in your experience. You know you are a child of God, you have trusted Jesus as your Savior, but maybe you are not quite out of the miry clay and, even if you are, your feet are not set firmly upon a rock. This is the experience of many Christians these days— saved, but still slipping!

The lesson, and the answer for us here is in the first three words: "I waited patiently." The word "waited" can have several meanings, and express several moods. There is the waiting which is really hanging around, putting in time. This is a completely negative experience, productive of nothing but boredom. Sad to say this is how some Christians approach their Christian life. They know their sins are forgiven, they know they have a home in heaven—and that is that. What more is there left to do, except to wait until they get to heaven and in the meantime try and do the best they can—when they remember and if they choose.

But the word "wait" in the original is a much more exciting word. It expresses the idea of expecting, looking for, hoping in a positive way. See how the whole Psalm is changed if we say: "I expected from the Lord; and he inclined unto me." There are many Christians who expect nothing more. Their idea is that salvation is a finished work—Jesus died, our sins are dealt with, we will go to heaven when we die, and that is all there is. So what is the point of getting excited and expecting something else, when it is all done! People who think that way and live that way, end up being bored to death. If we expect nothing, we will look for nothing, and we will surely find nothing!

God's salvation includes the finished work of Christ. Thank God we can read in Hebrews 10:12: "One sacrifice for sins for ever." Never again will Jesus die. By His glorious death He has procured for us forgiveness of our sins and the certain assurance of a place in heaven. This we believe, this is our hope and joy. But this is not all that God has for us in His tremendous plan of salvation.

The Bible speaks of the saving death of Christ, all that is ours because He died for us. Then it speaks, just as firmly, in Romans 5:10 of the saving life of Christ—all that can be ours because He indwells us by His Holy Spirit. The saving death of Christ is the finished work of Christ. The saving life of Christ is the glorious, continual unfolding experience of knowing His presence real in our hearts day by day.

Philippians 1:6 (Amplified Version) gives the same thought: "I am convinced *and* sure of this very thing, that He Who began a good work in you will continue until the day of Jesus Christ—right up to the time of His return—developing [that good work] *and* perfecting *and* bringing it to full completion in you." How true these words are—and God continues His good work through the indwelling Christ. Certainly there is the finished work of Christ, but thank God, just as certainly there is a continuing experience of being saved day by day.

It is this glorious unknown certainty to which we refer when we say: "I expected from the Lord." I can expect God to be true and faithful every moment of every day. I can expect all His promises to come true in my life. But I have to realize that: "For as many as are the promises of God, they all find their Yes (answer) in Him (Christ)" (2 Cor. 1:20, Amplified).

God has so much more for each one of us, if we will only make Christ real day by day and expect, by simple faith. Just as we expected God to be faithful at the cross, by the death of Christ, so we must expect God to be faithful in the crises of life, by the saving life of Christ. By faith, we should be able to take verse 5 in the Psalm and say: "Many, O Lord my God, are thy wonderful works which thou [*wilt* do] . . . they cannot be reckoned up in order unto thee."

When we turn to the next thought in the Psalm we see the price th Jesus paid in order to bring us this reality and this expectancy. Again we see the New Testament pointing to the Old Testament and saying: "Look, this is Jesus." Verses 6 to 8 in the Psalm say:

> *Sacrifice and offering thou didst not desire; mine ears hast thou opened: burnt offering and sin offering hast thou not required.*
>
> *Then said I, Lo, I come: in the volume of the book it is written of me,*
>
> *I delight to do thy will, O my God.*

Hebrews 10:5-7 makes a direct reference to these words, relating them all to Jesus. But there is one slight change we will see, and this is a treasury of truth in itself:

> *Wherefore when he cometh into the world, he saith, Sacrifice and offering thou wouldest not, but a body hast thou prepared me:*
>
> *In burnt offerings and sacrifices for sin thou hast had no pleasure.*
>
> *Then said I, Lo, I come (in the volume of the book it is written of me,) to do thy will, O God.*

There is a similarity in both these quotations, except for one area. Verse 6 in the Psalm says: "Mine ears hast thou opened." The corresponding phrase in Hebrews 10:5, 6: "A body hast thou prepared me." These two phrases, which imply the same resulting truth, have a deep and significant contrast to show us.

Let us look at the phrase in Psalm 40, "Mine ears hast thou opened." At first sight this does not make much sense. But when we look at the original word which is here translated "opened," we find the beginning of an exciting story. The original word really means "pierced"—"mine ears hast thou pierced." This whole passage is dealing with the story of the Christ who came to serve the Father and to do His will. It is in the context of this thought that we can find a meaning for the words, "Mine ears hast thou pierced."

We will find the answer in Exodus 21:1-6 and in Deuteronomy 15:12-17. Both of these passages are telling the story of "The Year of Release." God commanded in His law in Deuteronomy 15:1, "At the end of every seven years thou shalt make a release." This was called the Lord's release. Every creditor who had loaned money to a fellow Jew had to release the debtor from any further payment. Verse 12 goes on to say: "And if thy brother, an Hebrew man, or an Hebrew woman, be sold unto thee, and serve thee six years; then the seventh year thou shalt let him go free from thee.

"And when thou sendest him out free from thee, thou shalt not let him go away empty." The passage goes on to tell what gifts had to be given to the freed slave.

This may seem most unbusinesslike to us, according to modern practices, but this was God's way of leveling up and leveling down. If this was faithfully carried out there would never be great extremes of social practice and behavior in the Hebrew culture.

But God made provision for one unusual situation. There could be a slave who worked for a master who was wonderfully kind, honest, and gracious. Such a slave would know security and protection always. His master would provide for all his needs, care for him when he was sick or old, protect him from his enemies, and be to him the answer to his loneliness and longing.

When the seventh year drew near in which the slave could go free, he might view his prospective freedom with fear and uncertainty. To be free would mean being thrust out into a hard cruel world. For such a slave the answer to his greatest need would not be permanent freedom, but permanent security. So it was God provided a permanent way out from the fear of freedom.

Verses 16 and 17 tell of the strange ritual to be followed—the ritual of the pierced ear: "And it shall be, if he say unto thee, I will not go away from thee; because he loveth thee and thine house, because he is well with thee;

"Then thou shalt take an awl, and thrust it through his ear unto the door, and he shall be thy servant for ever. And also unto thy maidservant thou shalt do likewise."

Exodus 21:5, 6 tells of the same procedure, but in this case it mentions that the ritual had to be done in the presence of "the judges."

Once the slave had made the momentous decision to ask for the pierced ears, then his freedom was gone forever. He could choose the exciting uncertainty of freedom or the guaranteed security of peace and protection. This was indeed a challenge to any man or woman. But notice how the decision was to be made: "I will not go away from thee; because he loveth thee and thine house, because he is well with thee." It was based on love for the master and love for the house. The pierced ear was a dedication to the slavery of love for evermore.

This is the meaning of the phrase in Psalm 40. In prophetical language the Lord Jesus was offering Himself to His Father in total and unending service. There was to be no holding back and no turning back—"I delight to do thy will, O my God."

Now see the amazing contrast in Hebrews 10:5. Instead of the pierced ears we read: "but a body hast thou prepared me." The passage then goes on: "I come . . . to do thy will . . . By the which will we are sanctified through the offering of the body of Jesus Christ once for all." In an awesome way the pierced ears led on to the pierced hands and feet, to the pierced side. And all this was done in love to the Father and in obedience to His holy will.

Psalm 40 tells of the promise made, Hebrews 10 tells of the price paid.

First in this Psalm we considered the results, in our hearts and lives, of the experience of the love of God. Then we considered the cost of it all, the price paid by our blessed Lord.

Let us consider, finally, our own response to this wonderful salvation. Do you love your Lord and Master? Is it well with you in the house of your Lord and Master? Would you ever consider coming to Him and asking for the privilege of "the pierced ear" in your own life? Or do you still have a desire for freedom with all the excitement of a sure uncertainty? Are you missing something good by being a Christian? Of course, if you are not "expecting from the Lord" then there will be a sense of boredom in your Christian life, and freedom—so called—may seem to you to be the answer.

I have found, through the years, that where there is the sense of the fullness of Christ in the heart of a Christian—a counting on the saving life of Christ, day by day—then there is this daily sense of expectancy. The believer can truly say, "I expected from the Lord." Each day can begin with the thought, "Thank You, Lord, for the gift of this new day. Now what have You in store for me today?" This life brings a sense of joyous freedom never known before. I can live in total dependence on a Christ who knows where He is going, and how He is going to get there, and who wants me to go with Him.

To enjoy this to the full I, too, should come to my Master and ask for the privilege of the pierced ear. In doing so, I commit myself irrevocably to His ownership and to His will. I give up all rights to my own life in every area of living. I take my hands off completely. Forever after I have no more decisions to make, only commands to obey.

In return, I can count on that which the Hebrew slave enjoyed—security and protection, provision for all my need, care for me when I am sick or elderly, protection from my enemies, and the answer to my loneliness and longing. All this is mine in Christ, as I enjoy Him day by day.

This is not a wild dream, or a foolish philosophy. This is what God's salvation is—if only we will become involved.

Thousands of sincere Christians have come in days past to seek the privilege of the pierced ear. There is room for many more in this day and generation. Are you interested? Don't forget to count the cost—both ways!

12

Putting God in His Place

Psalm 132

This is a precious Psalm, full of historical interest, and it has a vital message for us today—all in relationship to the risen Christ and our involvement with Him.

These are the words David wrote when he had achieved his great ambition of getting the Ark of God into the city of Jerusalem. There was a background of sadness and failure extending over many years. Much had to happen and many lessons had to be learned before David eventually put God in His place. That is really what was happening. The Ark represented the presence of God in the religious arrangement of those days. God's plan given to Moses was that the Ark should be in the Holy of Holies within the tent of the Tabernacle, but failure in the priesthood had resulted in a total breakdown of God's plan.

This section of David's story begins in First Chronicles 11. The end of chapter 10 tells of the death of Saul due to his transgression against the word of the Lord. Then come these refreshing words in chapter 11: "Then all Israel gathered themselves to David unto Hebron, saying, Behold, we are thy bone and thy flesh . . . . Therefore came all the elders of Israel to the king to Hebron; and David made a covenant with them in Hebron before the Lord; and they anointed David king over Israel."

He had been king over Judah for seven and a half years, now he was to begin a glorious reign of thirty-three years over the whole of God's people. He moved his capital from Hebron to Jerusalem. Thus it was that Jerusalem became the great center of Jewish life and culture.

But one thing was missing—the presence of God. Psalm 132:3-5 gives us the longing desires of David's heart:

> *Surely I will not come into the tabernacle of my house, nor go up into my bed;*
>
> *I will not give sleep to mine eyes, or slumber to mine eyelids,*
>
> *Until I find out a place for the Lord, an habitation for the mighty God of Jacob.*

David had the kingdom. After years of struggling and suffering he was God's man in God's place at last. David had the city of his desires—Jerusalem was his to use for the glory of God. Now he wanted to possess the presence of God, so that he could go forward conscious always that God was with him.

So it is we read in First Chronicles 13:1-5:

> *And David consulted with the captains of thousands and hundreds, and with every leader.*
>
> *And David said unto all the congregation of Israel, If it seem good unto you, and that it be of the Lord our God, let us send abroad unto our brethren everywhere . . . that they may gather themselves unto us:*
>
> *And let us bring again the ark of our God to us: for we inquired not at it in the days of Saul.*
>
> *And all the congregation said they would do so: for the thing was right in the eyes of all the people.*
>
> *So David gathered all Israel . . . to bring the ark of God from Kirjath-jearim.*

Notice David's comment in verse 3: "We inquired not at it in the days of Saul." When Saul was king little consideration was paid to the Ark. It stood unused and neglected at Kirjath-jearim. What an unusual situation—a total neglect of the presence of God. See how this compares with David's eager desire to make God real in his life.

It is a fascinating story to see how the Ark of Go got to Kirjath-jearim in the first place. This again wa a case of lack of appreciation of the presence of Go

First Samuel 5 tells how the Philistines captured t holy Ark after Eli's two sons, Hophni and Phineh defied the law of God by taking it to the battlefie The Philistines at first were elated with their captu To them the Ark was just the God of the Jews, e as they had their own gods, such as Dagon. But began to pour out His judgments on the Philistine their abuse of His holy Ark, and they in turn beg seek to get rid of the awful object. In verse 8 cried: "What shall we do with the ark of the G Israel?" They tried passing it on to others o great cities, but no one wanted it—the danger w great!

After spending seven months in the land of the Philistines, the Ark was sent on its way. The priests and diviners of the Philistines devised a way to return the Ark. They made a new cart on which to carry the Ark and offered jewels of gold as a trespass offering. They put two cows to pull it, and sent it off on its own. To everyone's amazement the cows left their new calves and pulled the cart out of the land of the Philistines back into the territory of the Jews. So the Ark was once more in the land, but it did not get very far. The people of Bethshemesh showed no respect for it, and judgment fell on them. Everywhere it went the Ark brought trouble, because no one knew how to deal with this object of holy power.

Eventually, the Ark was taken to Kirjath-jearim, and there it stayed in the house of Abinadab. But this was a wrong situation and no real blessing came. True, the Ark was in the land, but it was in the wrong place and the wrong man was looking after it. First Samuel 7:1 records how Abinadab, who was of Judah and not a Levite, sanctified his son Eleazar to keep the Ark of the Lord. It stayed there for twenty years—out of place, out of relationship—and no one ever came to seek the mind of the Lord.

David knew all about this, and this is why his great desire was to put God back in His place, so that the nation would be blessed and God would be honored.

Thus in First Chronicles 13 David and the people went down to the house of Abinadab to bring up the Ark of God. David had the right desire, and he wanted to do the right thing, but the following verses show that he set about it the wrong way: "And they carried the ark of God in a new cart out of the house of Abinadab: and Uzza and Ahio drave the cart." This method of transport was that devised by the heathen priests and diviners over twenty years ago—this was not God's way of moving the holy Ark. They took it out in the same way as it came in—without seeking the mind of God.

Verse 8 records all the emotional excitement of the time: "And David and all Israel played before God with all their might, and with singing, and with harps, and with psalteries, and with timbrels, and with cymbals, and with trumpets." There was tremendous sincerity in all their hearts and great love and devotion to God, but it is not enough to be sincere—it must be done God's way.

The succeeding verses tell how the oxen stumbled as they pulled the cart, and how Uzza put forth his hand to steady the Ark: "and there he died before God." All the excitement vanished. The sincerity and devotion gave way to fear. David asked the same question that the Philistines had posed years before: "How shall I bring the ark of God home to me?" And this is how the day ended: "So David brought not the ark home to himself to the city of David, but carried it aside into the house of Obed-edom the Gittite." And there it stayed for three months while David set about finding the answer to his problem: "How shall I bring the ark of God home to me?"

First Chronicles 15 tells the happy ending to the many years of useless living. For all those years God was in the land, but no one came to seek His counsel, no one made God real. This is the beginning of the message to our hearts from this great Psalm. There are many Christians who also have "God in the land," but He is not real and His power is not known or experienced.

David found the answer to his question. You can see this in verses 1 and 2.

> *And David made him houses in the city of David, and prepared a place for the ark of God, and pitched for it a tent.*
>
> *Then David said, None ought to carry the ark of God but the Levites: for them hath the Lord chosen to carry the ark of God, and to minister unto him for ever.*

David had searched God's Word to find out how God had ordained for His Ark, and he found his answer in Numbers 7. Here we read how the Tabernacle and its contents were to be moved. It tells of six new carts and twelve oxen, but these were not for the Ark. Verse 9 says: "But unto the sons of Kohath he gave none: because the service of the sanctuary belonging unto them was that they should bear upon their shoulders."

Much of the Tabernacle material was to be carried in the carts, but the Ark and other similar holy vessels were to be carried on the shoulders of the Levites.

So in First Chronicles 15:12 and 13 David instructed the Levites to prepare:

> *Ye are the chief of the fathers of the Levites: sanctify yourselves, both ye and your brethren,*

that ye may bring up the ark of the Lord God of Israel unto the place that I have prepared for it.

For because ye did it not at the first, the Lord our God made a breach upon us, for that we sought him not after the due order.

This time they repeated all the excitement, all the music, all the singing—and it was all done according to the commandment of the Lord. This day was a great day in the life of David. The kingdom was his, the city of Jerusalem was his—and now, his great desire was fulfilled—God was in His proper place, in the midst of His people.

It is against this background that we read this great Psalm. David said in verses 6-8, referring to the Ark:

Lo, we heard of it at Ephratah: we found it in the fields of the wood.

We will go into his tabernacles: we will worship at his footstool.

Arise, O Lord, into thy rest; thou, and the ark of thy strength.

It is good to read the answer of the Lord to this desire in the heart of David. Verse 14 says: "This is my rest for ever: here will I dwell; for I have desired it." The Lord then went on to promise all the blessing that David was seeking. It is amazing to realize that this was the desire of the Lord also. God had no glory or honor while the Ark was left in Kirjath-jearim. No one sought God, and the land was starved of blessing. The people had no rest and God had no rest. But when God's people put God in His proper place then the doors were opened for unending blessing.

This is where the Psalm continues to speak to us. We who are true Christians have Christ indwelling us by His Holy Spirit. This is the proof of our faith. But with many of us, He is "in the land," but not in His proper place. As a result we have no rest, we have no sense of His presence and His power. Christ is equally without rest within us when we deny Him His proper place in our hearts and lives. There are many believers of whom it can be said, "they never inquired of him" in a vital way—because He, too, was in their land, but not where He ought to be.

There are some direct and powerful words for each one of us in Ephesians 3:14-21 concerning this very subject. Paul prays: "For this cause I bow my knees unto the Father of our Lord Jesus Christ, Of whom the whole family in heaven and earth is named."

Paul had this burden of prayer on his heart. This is the one thing he desired for these people: "That he would grant you, according to the riches of his glory, to be strengthened with might by his Spirit in the inner man." Notice the progression of involvement set forth in this prayer. First, Paul wanted them to have the reality of a conversion experience, such as we read of in Romans 8:16: "The Spirit himself beareth witness with our spirit, that we are the children of God." This, in a sense, brings God back into the land. But then Paul goes on: "That Christ may dwell in your hearts by faith." The Amplified Bible puts it this way: "May Christ through your faith [actually] dwell—settle down, abide, make His permanent home—in your hearts!"

This is putting Christ in His proper place—permanently settled in our hearts. David wanted the Ark at the center of his whole kingdom and this is where we need to know Christ real.

We can compare the errors they made in their relationship with the Ark with the kind of mistakes we make as Christians. First, they were content to have the Ark in the land. God was there inside the borders, and that was all that mattered. They had the respectable feeling of having God there, and then they lived their own lives their own way. There are many Christians whose lives are equally respectable, but totally useless and ineffective. They have the right Man, but they keep Him in the wrong place.

Another error they made was that they treated the

Ark with familiarity and carelessness. They were not wicked, just lacking in a sense of the holiness of God. Sometimes I feel we also get a little too familiar with God. The great lesson of the Old Testament is the holiness of God and man's relationship to that holiness. God is still as holy as He ever was. Our modern society which has thrown overboard so many standards and virtues can have a lowering effect upon our own standards of holiness with regard to almighty God.

The greatest mistake David made was that of copying the plan of the heathen priests. Like them he made a new cart and set out to follow their example. He was doing the right thing the wrong way. I meet Christians who seek also to do the right thing, to draw closer to God, but they do it the wrong way. They look for a new experience, a new way, something they can do and construct, something on which they can "carry Christ"—taking Him with them, getting carried along on the excitement.

God's plan was to have two staves of wood, one going through rings on one side of the Ark and the other going through rings on the other side. Two pieces of wood borne on the shoulders of God's chosen men carried the Ark, the reality of the presence of God. These two pieces of wood remind me of the cross—it also was made of two pieces of wood, and it was borne on the shoulders of God's chosen man, as He dragged His way to Calvary.

If I want to put Christ in His place in my life, I must step aside and yield the throne of my heart to Him. Not just a temporary visitor to help me through a time of testing, but so that He can settle down and make His permanent home in my heart and life—Jesus in the midst.

When Jesus has His proper place, then I can know His peace, His power, and His rest. The blessings of God will be seen in my life. I will inquire of Him and seek His will. All this can, and will, be mine. if only I will do the right thing in the right way.

13

How to Build a Home — and a Church

Psalm 127

There is much talk today of finding new ways to make the Church strong and vigorous. One of the obvious ways used and discussed is the amalgamation of groups and denominations. The reason being, "the more we are together the stronger we will be." This makes good sense in the eyes of the world. This is good business practice, companies uniting to pool their resources and to cut down their overhead expenses.

This would be an excellent idea, except for one fact —the Church is not a business. In the eyes of God, and in the light of the Scriptures, it is the Body of Christ. The unity already exists within the Body. The Church is not an organization but an organism. There is also only one Body. Just as Jesus is *the* way, *the* truth, and *the* life so the Church is the Body.

Improvement to a body does not come from without, but from within. A good medical doctor does not treat the symptoms of a man's illness as individual items to be dealt with one at a time. He examines the symptoms and uses them as a guide to help him diagnose the illness. Successful diagnosis is essential to successful treatment.

One other important thing to remember is that the Lord builds His Church with families—and not with individuals. This is something we seem to have forgotten these days—the importance of the family in the life of the Church. I have been much impressed lately, as I have been in the Orient, to see the way many of the pastors and missionaries have been gripped with this idea. They concentrate on winning families to Christ. This is their aim, their prayer and their whole purpose.

I was in a church in Keelung, Taiwan, recently, and the pastor spoke of his growing church. He did not refer to this man or this woman—he spoke of this family that joined, and then, that family that joined. He was not satisfied with the man or the woman, his aim was the family—all one in Christ—and God was rewarding his faith.

A church is as strong as its families are strong. Communism recognizes this fact, that families are the "bricks" with which God builds His Church and His world. This is why the communists seek, first of all, to break down the structure of family life. Every country which falls into their hands is subjected to this relentless power of family destruction. It is often possible to recognize the importance of a quality or a structure in the eyes of God by the way the communist doctrine seeks to crush or devaluate that item. Witness their devaluation of truth, peace, love—all basic qualities in the economy of God—all distorted and destroyed in the doctrine of satanic communism.

Some of our large and well-organized churches seeking, by all means, to improve their appeal and their image, are doing so at the expense of the family. They have missed the important fact that God builds His Church with families, and not with organizations within the church. I have been to churches which have a tremendous program laid out through the week. If the various members of a family took their full part in such a program, some of them would never see each other—not even on Sunday mornings!

Notice the importance of the Christian home in the days of the early Church—the home *was* the Church.

They had no special buildings set aside to be used for church worship and church activities. The church met in the home. Romans 16:3 and 5 says: "Greet Priscilla and Aquila my helpers in Christ . . . Likewise greet the church that is in their house." This couple was at that time living in Rome, and the Church met in their house. Compare this with First Corinthians 16:19, which was written from Philippi: "The churches of Asia salute you. Aquila and Priscilla salute you much in the Lord, with the church that is in their house." This dear couple was by then living in Philippi, but they had a church meeting in their home again. This is real home Bible studies!

Colossians 4:15 tells us: "Salute the brethren which are in Laodicea, and Nymphas, and the church which is in his house." Philemon 2 adds: "And to our beloved Apphia, and Archippus our fellow-soldier, and to the church in thy house."

This does not suggest, for one moment, that the modern use of specially designated buildings is unscriptural or out of place. The Jewish Christians used the synagogue at first when it was available to them, and Paul used the school of Tyrannus day after day as a place in which to preach the Word of God (Acts 19:9). God has blessed and honored the use of church buildings down through the ages. We need to distinguish between the Church, the one Church, the one Body of Christ and the church, the local group meeting in the local building, which is a part of the Body of Christ.

Recognizing then the importance of the home, we need to find out what the Bible has to say about it. Any truth and teaching from the Scriptures which will help strengthen the home is vital to the life of the church. Psalm 127 has much to say in this connection. We can link this Psalm once more with the words of our Lord in Luke 24:44: "All things must be fulfilled, which were written . . . in the psalms, concerning me." We have been finding Jesus in the Psalms. Wherever we find the risen Christ we find reality, we find His presence and His power and His peace. As we study this Psalm, which is teaching the basic essentials for building a home in God's way, we will once more recognize the living Christ. If we can only get the risen Christ in the home, and keep Him in the home, and see His relevance to the day-by-day running of the home—then blessing is inevitable in all areas.

This Psalm begins with *the* most important truth in building a home: "Except the Lord build the house, they labor in vain that build it." It is a truth so simple in its telling, but so difficult in the doing. This verse is teaching us that there is only one builder in the home, and that builder is God. In like manner there are those who are called laborers—the husband and the wife. It is at this initial point that we can see the seeds of all future failure in a Christian home. There is only one builder. He devised the plans because He is the architect as well as the builder. He knows exactly what He wants to do in the lives of the Christian couple.

Remember that the phrase "a Christian home," presupposes that the husband and wife are real Christians. I heard of someone who said their home was a Christian home because they had an old Bible in a box somewhere in the house! Because we are Christians, real Christians, then we are not our own. "Ye are not your own? For ye are bought with a price: therefore glorify God in your body, and in your spirit, which are God's" (1 Cor. 6:19, 20). We glorify God only when we obey Him. And we are told to glorify Him in our bodies as well as in our spirits. Just as our bodies live in our homes so we are to obey Him there. We do this as we recognize Him as the builder. What He says, goes!

In just the same way the Bible speaks of the husband and wife as the laborers—those whose job it is to carry out the plans and desires of the builder. This is the chief area of all failure in the marriage relationship—the failure to see ourselves as laborers, simply common laborers, whose job it is to keep at it, day by day, in heat and cold, in rain and fire. It is so much easier to be a boss and sit in the office!

See what this first verse says—if you don't labor, then it is all in vain. The phrase "in vain" means you put in a lot of hours, spend a lot of time, use a lot of energy, waste a lot of money, and at the end, you have nothing to show. It is just a dead loss.

Someone will say, "But isn't the husband the head of the house?" The answer to that is, certainly he is the head of the house, he is the head laborer!

So often in the early days of a marriage there is a silent, secret struggle for power. The husband is determined to be the head, the boss. The wife thinks, "Am I going to let this man boss me for the rest of my life?" This is the natural desire of a fallen human nature with its lust for independence at all costs.

I see many homes where the husband, glorying in his position as head of the house, assumes the position of builder and architect. He says what he wants done, and where, and how. Then, carrying out his role as builder, he leaves the hard grind of laboring to his wife. I have listened to young married women cry as they recount the hours of toil left all to them. It is not that they object to the work. What irks them is to see the husband evading the responsibility and leaving the "blood, toil, tears and sweat" to them. As one such woman said, "I conceived the children, carried the children, bore the children—then he leaves me to raise them, discipline them and fight it out all on my own." Such an arrangement in any home where there is only one laborer, is destined to be in vain.

Sometimes it is not the man who evades the laboring. There are some wives who build themselves a little kingdom in which they are the queen—who never gets off her throne, never takes off her crown—who issues orders to an adoring, laboring husband. If this goes on too long, there is nothing ahead but tragedy and failure.

Failure is inevitable if there is not one Builder and two laborers. Another point of tremendous importance is to remember that God is always building. Philippians 1:6 says: "Being confident of this very thing, that he which hath begun a good work in you will perform it (or continue it) until the day of Jesus Christ." The Bible says that God neither slumbers nor sleeps. His plan for our lives and for our home is an unfolding plan—there is always more to come—and the best is yet to be.

Because God is always building, then we must be always laboring. If you do not keep on laboring, then it will be in vain. The only way to build a successful Christian home is to work at it, and *keep on* working at it!

I want to suggest three special areas in which the laboring must be absolutely sincere and kept up to date. First there must be "a continual application to the task." This is of vital importance especially in the area of love and tender demonstration. We can assume in nearly every case, in a western marriage, that the husband and wife love each other at the beginning of their married life. I say "in a western marriage," because I am writing these words in the Orient where in some cases the marriage is still arranged by the parents. (Incidentally, it is surprising to see how these relationships, although not built on the passionate love so "essential" to our western mind, prove successful. This may be one of the reasons for their long-term success.)

The great tragedy in marriage is when this tender love is allowed to turn first into a limited affection, then later to lapse into a mutual recognition of two persons living in the same house. This so easily happens under the pressures of modern life. We are creatures of habit. We form habits both good and bad as a matter of course. Our tragedy is when tender love becomes a habit, for then it ceases to be tender, and it ceases to be love. The curse of the "habit" relationship is that we take each other for granted. It is not that we hate the other person, or dislike him, or that we are in any way against him. Our attitude is not negative, just neutral.

I remember a woman speaking to me at a couples' conference in California some time ago. I knew the couple well and recognized them as a happy couple in every way. One day the wife, who was in her middle forties, poured out her heartache. "John," she said, "my husband doesn't love me anymore." With these words she broke down into tears of deep grief. I assured her he was a fine man, an excellent husband in every way. With this she fully agreed, but this wasn't her problem. "I know he is good to me, and all that. My problem is that he takes me for granted. I'm just like a piece of mobile furniture in the house. He never tells me he loves me, never shows me any affection—" and so she continued. She was starving from the lack of simple, tender love.

I spoke to her husband later. I asked him if he loved his wife. "Of course I do," he replied. "I always have." What he said was perfectly true. I asked him when was the last time he had told her that he really loved her—in the way he used to do, years ago. "Oh," he said, "you don't do that when you've been married twenty years." I went on to explain to him the emptiness in his marriage, the danger to his marriage and how simple it was to correct it at this stage.

Later on that week the wife came to me with her face lit up with radiant joy. "John," she cried, "he loves me. He told me so himself." It was a work of divine healing to see the warm glow of love blossom between these two once more. We prayed together, each for each. They recognized anew the fact of the indwelling Christ. They put Him where He belonged. They took their proper place. They yielded all to Him—then they went back to the same house, but to a different home! They were working at the task of maintaining their marriage. God was building and they were laboring.

As a woman grows older, and she loses her youth,

she loses those special qualities of looks and appearance that made her especially attractive to "him." As she loses these, she often loses her confidence in herself. At such a time she needs all the extra loving and tender devotion that can make her feel desired and loved and "special." But so often when this time of need develops, she has reached the "being taken for granted" stage—with all its cold deadness and empty existence. This is why we are emphasizing the continual application to the task. This is the husband's job—no one can do it for him. He is the laborer, and this is his task. It does not require diamonds or mink—just tender love and simple devotion—expressed in the many ways possible.

In like manner, when the husband gets older he, too, loses his looks and his figure—often more so than the wife. The fine, upstanding, athletic young man who swept you off your feet has lost his capacity to sweep! His shape is altered, his hair line is altered, his constant sparkle is reduced to an occasional twinkle. But he is still a boy at heart—every man is really a little boy grown up. Even though he would not say so, he needs all the appreciation and encouragement you can give him as a wife, more so as the years go by. If you, as his wife, do not give him that appreciation and encouragement, he may seek it somewhere else, from someone else. This is the time when some older men seek feminine friendships elsewhere. It is not basically because they want to be unfaithful, but because they want to be appreciated in some way, for some purpose.

Psalm 127:1 says, "Except the Lord build the house, they labor in vain that build it." The Lord is always building, but are you always laboring?

14

Laborers Wanted – Apply Within

Psalm 127

We finished the last chapter by discussing the first special area in which the laboring must be absolutely sincere and kept up-to-date. Let us now look at the second of such areas—still in connection with the initial thought of this Psalm, that God is the one Builder, that the husband and wife are the laborers, and inasmuch as they cease to labor, in that much the marriage is in vain.

This second special area is in "a continual adjustment to circumstances." These are the circumstances that make up the stuff of daily living. The adjustment can be a development in the boring things of life, a continuing experience in the ordinary, or majoring in the mundane.

Most marriages follow the pattern set by others. First, there is the build-up of excitement as the "Great Day" arrives. Then the explosion of love, as the couple go "into orbit." The honeymoon follows, during which both learn to walk on cloud nine—no one in the world exists but you—nothing in the world exists but you. You are up there, walking in space.

Then, sooner or later, the descent begins as the husband and wife seek to adjust to the inevitable issues of daily living. It is amazing how soon, in some cases, "cloud nine" can be followed by "basement seven" where the cold shock of truth causes much re-thinking. This is the time when the continual adjustment to circumstances must be carried out. This is where the laboring begins in earnest—but remember, God is still building.

This is when the couple see each other as they really are—with the masks off, and no holds barred. This is the time when you turn the coin over, and see what is on the other side! Things you never imagined come to light—weaknesses, unpleasant habits, noises, smells, irritations—and it is all true. And all the time the key word is "adjustment"—continual adjustment.

As life goes on the first baby appears, and this demands tremendous adjustment in every area. If there is no willingness to adjust, then the seeds are sown for future failure. The husband must adjust his schedule, the wife has to adjust her daily and hourly program. Yet this is what marriage is, working at it. It is recognizing that indwelling you both is the Christ who said He would never leave you; thanking Him, together, for the wonder of His love and the glory of His giving; always trusting in Him, resting in His presence and His power, and adjusting to the changing tide of life.

More babies follow, and now the battle is on in real earnest as less time is left for selfish things. This is where cracks start to appear in the marriage. Someone asks, even silently, "Why should I give up so much, all the time? Other people don't, why should I?" This is the time when it is good to be a committed Christian, for now the challenge in your life is being raised. You are tested as never before, not by the enemy around you, but by the self within. Acceptance from the hands of Christ and adjustment to the pattern of living is the only answer.

And so the years go by, babies become juniors, juniors grow older, until you have teenagers. Some of you reading these words are struggling in the Teenage Jungle, sometimes wondering why you ever had children, or, for that matter, why you ever married. If

Christ has grown dearer to you as the years have gone by, then He will be nearer to you day by day. This is where husband and wife need more than ever to make Christ real in their daily lives—both personally and together. These are days when you can prove Him real in many new ways, always as you rest in Him and keep adjusting to the circumstances.

One of the greatest tests in a marriage comes after the children have left home. This is what I call coming back to "square one." This is where you started off—just the two of you. This is where you find out whether you have been living—or just existing. If Christ has been real to you both as the years have passed, then this is where you reap the harvest of new love and adventure together. As you have adjusted and labored together, so you have been welded together in the crucible of life. It will not be a case of two strangers alone in an empty house, but two sweethearts together, with a new oneness in Christ and a new freedom to love Him and to serve Him together.

Where God is the only builder and the husband and wife are the constant laborers, each phase of a marriage seems the best, as you reach it. It is the best at the beginning. It is the best with one baby, the best with more babies, with the young children. A new kind of best comes with the teens. A better best can be yours on square one again. This is always so when the living, risen Christ is in control. He always brings reality; He always provides sufficiency. We can keep on saying with Peter in Matthew 17:4: "Lord, it is good for us to be here."

There is one other adjustment that may be necessary, and this is the one that hurts and keeps on hurting. The wonderful "two" may become the lonely "one," and you find yourself alone for the first time in—how many years was it? It can come to any of us, but even then it is possible to adjust within the framework of His love. Jesus will not leave us, for He is faithful who promised. It is still possible through the tears of a breaking heart to raise the challenge of First Corinthians 15:55: "O death, where is thy sting? O grave, where is thy victory?" It is still possible to claim the promise of verse 57: "But thanks be to God, which giveth us the victory through our Lord Jesus Christ." The empty hand of faith can always claim and hold fast the promises of God.

Verse 58 of this same chapter provides an appropriate verse for our present line of thinking: "Therefore, my beloved brethren, be ye stedfast, unmovable, always abounding in the work of the Lord, forasmuch as ye know that your labor is not in vain in the Lord." Notice, it is the work of the Lord—the One who is the builder, and your labor is not in vain!

There is a third special area in which the laboring must be constant. This follows on from that with which we have just been dealing. It is "a continual acceptance of situation." This, in a sense, is not the natural development of circumstances which flow through each and every married life. These are the situations which burst upon us without warning, that come without any seeking, and often leave us baffled as to how to cope with them. These may include tragedies, disasters, bereavements. Things that cause even the world to stop and notice—for a few moments!

There are two things, basically, we can do in such circumstances. When the initial shock has come and registered deep in our hearts, we can either accept it, or fight it. Much will depend upon our attitude to the will of God. If we see the will of God as something stern, forbidding, almost negative in its dealing, then we may develop reactions of tense resistance. These reactions can become seeds which in time produce the roots of bitterness which in time flower into resentments and hostilities.

If, on the other hand, we are really taught in the Word, then we know that the "will of God is the love of God in action." This can never be understood at the time—only as the years pass and we sometimes see that it was the good and perfect will of God. It is by faith alone that we accept the situation which causes the heartache and the utter destruction of our hopes and dreams. Written on paper these words look so cold and insufficient. We just thank God that His will and His love are not words on paper, but the warm presence of Christ in our lives day by day.

Recently I was in Viet Nam. I was speaking with a brave and noble lady whose life has challenged me more than all else has over recent years. She is a missionary. Nine years ago her husband was taken prisoner by the Viet Cong as he was working in the hospital. She and some of her children were with him at the time. Since that day she has not heard from him, in any way. She has heard rumors and stories that he is yet alive, but she has an assurance from God in her heart that this is so. She looks and longs for the day of his release. God grant that this may be soon!

She told me how, at first, the shock caused bitterness and bewilderment in her heart. But then there came a day when, by faith, she accepted this whole situation. She saw that God could be using her husband in a unique way as he moved among the enemy. It was the fact and the quality of her acceptance that moved me so much. She was claiming a victory in Christ and the fruits of that victory were to be seen in her quiet manner and her demonstration of the measure of the stature of the fullness of Christ.

Over the last few years the Lord has given me the privilege of meeting and knowing other blessed men and women who have also found a new quality of life through the acceptance of situations which would otherwise have soured or seared their work and witness. In sharp contrast I remember a woman who spoke to me in a conference some time ago in California. She said she had never forgiven God for what He did to her years ago. He had taken her only child, a little girl. All the bitter flowers of resentment were in bloom in her life as she said, "I'll never forgive God for what

He did to me!" She looked exactly what she was—a bitter, joyless, resentful woman. Not a sign of inward or outward beauty was visible, just the ugly fruit of the root of bitterness. All because she had never accepted the will of God as the love of God.

There is another situation I would like to share with you. Some time ago at a couples' conference, I had been stressing as usual the importance of the role of the husband in the upbringing of the family. At the end of the conference two ladies came to me seeking help and advice. They said they were both divorcees. Their marriages had broken down, their husbands had gone, and they were both left with a family to raise. They wanted to know what the Bible had to say to help women in such situations.

They were not widows, in the sense that their husbands were dead, but they were alone with all the problems to handle by themselves. This situation is becoming increasingly so, as even in Christian homes there is a growing use of divorce as the only cure for a marriage which is full of tension. So many of these marriages could have been saved if the partners had been willing to accept the role of laborers responsible to God the only builder.

I went on to share some thoughts with these two ladies, and let me share them with you now. There are two words in the Bible which are both translated by the one English word "widow." The word in the New Testament is *chera* which means the bereaved one. This is the normal use we have of the word widow. The other word is in the Old Testament, it is the word *almanah*. The actual meaning of this Hebrew word is "the silent one," "the desolate one," "the forsaken one." This woman is not necessarily a widow in the sense that her husband is dead—she is alone, desolate and forsaken.

We know that divorce was allowed and practiced in the Old Testament days. In one sense it was much easier and much quicker to obtain. So there must have been many women who were widows, using the Old Testament definition.

It is interesting to see what the Bible has to say about these lonely women. There are many references to them and the word is generally linked with two other groups: "the stranger, the fatherless, and the widows." The Bible teaches that these unfortunate ones are in God's special care. Exodus 22:22, 23 says, "Ye shall not afflict any widow, or fatherless child. If thou afflict them in any wise, and they cry at all unto me, I will surely hear their cry."

Deuteronomy 10:18 tells how "He doth execute the judgment of the fatherless and widow, and loveth the stranger, in giving him food and raiment."

Deuteronomy 27:19 says, "Cursed be he that preventeth the judgment of the stranger, fatherless, and widow. And all the people shall say, Amen."

Psalm 68:5: "A father of the fatherless, and a judge of the widow, is God in his holy habitation."

Psalm 146:9: "The Lord preserveth the strangers; he relieveth the fatherless and widow."

These verses, and many more, all indicate one thing, that God has a special love and care and interest in widows—in lonely women with fatherless children. God is still the same; His love is ever true. These widows were told to cast themselves on the Lord, then He would protect them. This is the teaching of God's Word today for all such lonely forsaken women.

It is a precious thing to realize that the Lord Jesus has an intimate and actual knowledge of the sorrows and testings that come to a lonely woman. We know that Joseph died before the family of Mary had left home. We know that Jesus was the head of that little home in Nazareth. We know He stayed with Mary until He was thirty years old—all these facts are in the gospel story. It is easy to see that the other children of Mary would marry and leave home—this would be just the normal custom.

It is possible that Jesus spent the last of His thirty

years in Nazareth living in the home with Mary on her own. This is borne out by the way He committed His mother to His disciple John. John 19:26, 27 records: "When Jesus therefore saw his mother, and the disciple standing by, whom he loved, he saith unto his mother, Woman, behold thy son!

"Then saith he to the disciple, Behold thy mother! And from that hour that disciple took her unto his own home."

John, of course, was the one writing the account—about himself. The Lord Jesus committed His mother to John, who then took her into his own home. The implication is that previous to that, Mary had stayed in the old family home in Nazareth with Jesus coming to see her as and when He could.

Whichever way it was, we know that the Lord stayed on with His mother for many years, caring for her, loving her, understanding her. There is something unusually wonderful in realizing that this same Jesus is still the One who cares, whose heart is still moved with compassion toward widows and all lonely, forsaken women.

Thus, to those of you who have this burden of loneliness, the Bible brings its message of a God who cares and protects, and of a Savior who knows by experience the sorrow that hurts, and who comes with His heart full of compassion.

15

How to Ruin Your Children – and How Not To!

Psalm 127

In the last two chapters we have been concerned with the first half of verse 1 of this Psalm: "Except the Lord build the house, they labor in vain that build it." We have seen this in relation to the risen Christ who indwells by His Holy Spirit. We have seen Christ as the one builder; the husband and wife as the two laborers.

Now I want to show you how, in the second half of this same verse, we have a new emphasis. This time it is not building a home, but keeping a home. The subsequent verses tell us that we can see this in relation to children in the home.

Notice the similarity in both halves of the verse: "Except the Lord keep the city, the watchman waketh but in vain." Just as in the first half there was only one builder, so, in the second, there is only one keeper. If the Lord is not the keeper then, once again, the whole thing is in vain—it is useless. See how verse 2 brings in the same emphasis of uselessness in the marriage experience: "It is vain for you to rise up early, to sit up late, to eat the bread of sorrows: for so he giveth his beloved sleep."

Verse 2 spells out what happens in a home if there is not the total dependence on God, first as the only builder, then as the only keeper. These two experiences, building and keeping, run together. Wherever you find a married couple who have not made God the one builder, you will find the same couple trying to keep that which they have built. They may be absolutely sincere in all that they have planned and constructed, but the Bible, and experience, prove that inasmuch as God is left out, in that much there is uselessness and future failure.

It may seem a smooth and happy situation at the first when the children are small. You have the enthusiasm and the hope and the simple faith in your own ability. After all, you have read the right books on how to bring up the family, and you are sure you can make a success of this. But, I have met families where verse 2 is a horrible reality—where parents do rise up early, and do sit up late, and where they eat the bread of sorrows. The bread of sorrows is the daily diet of many Christian parents whose children are growing up. With the bread of sorrows goes the water of affliction, as the same parents face the "vanity," the hopeless waste, the pitiful and wretched situation in which they find themselves.

That is why I feel this Psalm has a great deal to say to many people—if they will only listen. Remember the basic rule—there must be only one builder, there must be only one keeper and He must be in command, His word must be obeyed. If not, it will all be in vain.

At the outset we should realize that before the Lord "keeps" the home, He must "keep" the parents. The word "keep" has an interesting history. In England during the times of the Normans, and on into the thirteenth and fourteenth centuries, many castles were built. Some of these castles are still standing exactly as they were when they were built. Some are even lived in today by families using them as an ordinary home.

These castles were erected as places of strength and protection. Around them was a high wall and on the top of this wall were places to walk, and turrets from which to aim arrows and other weapons. In the center of the space surrounded by the wall was a tall building of unusual strength. This was the final place of defense if the invaders broke through the gates or mounted the walls. This strong, rugged tower of defense was called "the Keep." It provided maximum protection by its thick wall and iron doors. It had a well within, reaching down to an endless supply of water. It was possible to hold out for weeks, months, or even years, if you were safe within the Keep and had a good supply of provisions.

It is this idea we can bear in mind as we say: "Except the Lord keep." If He keeps then we have all the protection, all the power and all the provisions necessary. Let us think of this fact—before the Lord keeps the home, He must first keep the parents. We can see this clearly stated in Isaiah 26. This chapter is teaching the reality of peace in human experience. Verse 3 speaks of the promise of peace. Verse 12 tells of the power for peace. Verses 13 and 14 tell of the program for peace.

Look at verse 3: "Thou wilt keep him in perfect peace, whose mind is stayed on thee: because he trusteth in thee." This is one of the greatest promises in the Bible, loved and enjoyed by all Christians. It is interesting, when thinking of the promises of God, to recall Second Corinthians 1:20: "For as many as are the promises of God, they all find their Yes (answer) in Him (Christ)" (Amplified). What a tremendous thought—all the promises of God find their *yes* in Christ. Wherever you see a promise in God's Word, and you wish that this could be yours, the answer is: It can be years, because all the promises of God find their *yes* in Christ.

If you read this third verse again, and see it in relation to the risen, victorious Christ who actually indwells you in the Person of His Holy Spirit, then here is the promise of peace, perfect peace. It also gives you the two necessary conditions. First, your mind is stayed on Christ—this is the fixed point of your faith. Then you keep on trusting in Him day by day—this is the continual application of your faith in any and all circumstances. It is not enough to have only the fixed point of faith in Christ as you trust Him at the cross. That will save you from your sins and guarantee you a home in heaven—praise God for that. But there are many Christians who have this fixed point of faith in Christ, who are truly saved, and yet their daily lives are a demonstration of fear, worry and uncertainty. They have been stayed but they are not daily trusting.

We are stayed at the cross as we rest in the finished work of Christ, His saving death. But then Romans 5:10 tells us that, beyond this experience, we can be daily delivered from sin's dominion by His risen life, as He indwells us. This is where the daily trusting comes in. This is where and when the risen Christ can keep us in perfect peace. He can also continue to keep us in perfect peace as we keep on trusting in Him—as He indwells us, never to leave us or forsake us.

Verse 12 goes on to show us this power for peace: "Lord, thou wilt ordain peace for us: for thou also hast wrought all our works in us."

How clearly this is stated—"thou wilt — for thou hast." This is the assurance of the power. As He works all our works in us then we have the continued guarantee of peace. We see the same thought in Philippians 2:13: "For it is God who is all the while effectually at work in you—energizing and creating in you the power and desire—both to will and to work for His good pleasure *and* . . . delight" (Amplified).

Notice once more that this assurance of the power for peace is based solely on the out-working of the indwelling Christ. When He is the one builder and the one keeper, then we enjoy the perfect peace. It also says, "Thou also hast wrought all our works in us"—

all our works, not some of them. The more we do, the less peace there is, the more vanity there is. The Word of God is so clear and honest in its teaching.

Verse 13 and 14 give us the program we must follow if we want this continuing peace in our hearts:

> *O Lord our God, other lords beside thee have had dominion over us: but by thee only will we make mention of thy name.*
>
> *They are dead, they shall not live; they are deceased, they shall not rise: therefore hast thou visited and destroyed them, and made all their memory to perish.*

This is referring to our past life, our past habits, sins and failures. Once they had dominion over us, and controlled our thoughts, our words, and our deeds. When we came to know Christ as our Savior, all these sins and evil deeds were forgiven. We have peace with God through our Lord Jesus Christ. But the problem with many Christians, young and old, is that although they have accepted Christ as their Savior at the cross, they have not made Him Lord of their life.

The program for peace is to make Jesus the Lord of your life, not only in words but in actual fact. If He is not Lord, then we cannot say: "They are dead, they shall not live." We may say so, in as many words, but, if we are not walking with Christ yielding all to Him, the old sins and habits and failures will move into our lives once more.

This is the way it is in some Christian homes, perhaps even in your home. You know for sure that you are saved, but there are habits unchecked, past lusts still pandered to, a few choice areas in your life not yielded to Christ. You think that you can indulge in these areas as and when you please. You think you can control these remnants of your old life. The Bible says: "Know ye not, that to whom ye yield yourselves servants to obey, his servants ye are to whom ye obey" (Rom. 6:16). If you indulge in these things then you become servants to these things and you must admit in all honesty that: "Other lords beside thee [*do* have] dominion over us."

I have counseled with many Christians who confess to areas of impurity in their lives, in some cases because they like it and enjoy it. Be sure of this, if these things are not nailed to the cross, if Christ is not given complete control of all, then He is not being allowed to be the one keeper. If He does not keep you, then He cannot keep your home. Some parents live their lives as they choose, then expect Christ to keep the family safe and sound.

Paul said in Second Timothy 1:12: "For I know whom I have believed, and am persuaded that he is able to keep that which I have committed unto him." In other words, He keeps what I commit. If I choose to keep it and deal with it myself, then it is my responsibility. If I commit it to Him, then He guarantees to be responsible. This goes for sin, self, sorrow, suffering and the whole range of human experience.

Thus we can see how desperately important it is—for our family's sake—to know the living Christ in all His personal keeping power. When we enter into this deepening relationship, as husband and wife, then we can confidently expect that He will keep our home and our children. He is faithful who promised.

The end of Psalm 127:2 teaches a truth that once was respected in America, but now it is being increasingly forgotten: "The watchman waketh but in vain." This is referring to the protection of the home from all outside influences that would harm or hinder. Notice that the word is "watchman" and not "watchwoman."

The Bible teaches that the husband is the head of the house—the head laborer! As such it is his duty to protect the home and guard his wife and children from the enemy. Every man is ready and prepared to give battle to any physical enemy that might attack his wife or his children, but this is not enough. There are enemies, far greater than thieves and bullies, seeking to break in and destroy every Christian home. Satan hates to see a happy home where Christ is honored and obeyed. We have already noticed how satanic communism seeks first of all to destroy the human family as a unit for love and mutual growth.

This is why the Bible speaks of a husband as a watchman, someone who is constantly on the lookout for an enemy which may break in. Many men leave this area of family planning to the wife. She is with the children, he is out so much, he is too busy—a thousand excuses can easily be manufactured to prove that looking after the home is the work of the wife. But the Bible speaks of a watchman and not a watchwoman.

Isaiah 56:10-12 is a graphic picture of how some men failed God in their responsibilities:

> *His watchmen are blind: they are all ignorant, they are all dumb dogs, they cannot bark; sleeping, lying down, loving to slumber.*
>
> *Yea, they are greedy dogs which can never have enough, and they are shepherds that cannot understand: they all look to their own way, every one for his gain, from his quarter.*
>
> *Come ye, say they, I will fetch wine, and we will fill ourselves with strong drink; and to-morrow shall be as this day, and much more abundant.*

This is a pitiful picture of men involved in materialism, whose only thought is for themselves. Some of these descriptions could be applied to some fathers—watchmen who are blind, dumb and careless.

Ezekiel 33:2-6 teaches what was the duty of a watchman in Israel's history:

> *If the people of the land take a man of their coasts, and set him for their watchman:*
>
> *If when he seeth the sword come upon the land, he blow the trumpet, and warn the people;*
>
> *Then whosoever heareth the sound of the trum-*

pet, and taketh not warning; if the sword come, and take him away, his blood shall be upon his own head.

He heard the sound of the trumpet, and took not warning; his blood shall be upon him. But he that taketh warning shall deliver his soul.

But if the watchman see the sword come, and blow not the trumpet, and the people be not warned; if the sword come, and take any person from among them, he is taken away in his iniquity; but his blood will I require at the watchman's hand.

These words are very challenging. They show the solemn responsibility of the watchman. If he does not watch and warn, then he is responsible and "his blood will I require at the watchman's hand."

Some fathers who have chosen to evade their responsibilities will have much to answer for to their Lord at the Judgment Seat of Christ.

How can a watchman do his work today? A watchman is what we would call a sentry. There are sentries on duty today in Viet Nam—young men who watch day and night for any sight or sound of the enemy. When they are suspicious they challenge the intruder to identify himself. If they recognize the enemy they do not rush out to attack on their own. They call in all the forces they have at their disposal on land or in the air. Their job is not so much to fight, as to watch and warn.

This is still the work of a watchman in the context of the Christian family. He looks out for the enemy seeking to get into the home. Satan comes in many amazing ways—books, magazines, "friends," TV programs, radio programs, habits, laziness. A father should know what is happening in his own home, and he should be able to discern the pure from the impure.

This does not, in any way, suggest that the home should be only for hymns and prayers—far from it!

There are plenty of good wholesome things to bring into a home, which provide all the fun and excitement necessary. There are family activities for all ages that produce a "togetherness" that give happy memories down through the years. The trouble is, in many cases today the home is a place from which we depart, not a center to which we come.

Some men have told me they are too busy at work to watch their family. If this is the case then they are just "too busy." Nothing in this world can justify the gradual breakdown of a Christian home.

Psalm 127:3 says: "Lo, children are an heritage of the Lord." They may be your children, but they also belong to God. God has loaned them to you, so that you can raise them for Him — they are His heritage. You are responsible to God, not for the success of your business activities, but for the success of your family. No excuse is permitted for slackness in this area.

When the father recognizes the enemy seeking to break in, he, too, does what the sentry does in Viet Nam. He calls in all the support he can find, on land and in the air. He and his wife make this an earnest matter of prayer as they seek Him who is able to keep. They commit the thing to Christ, and are not afraid to take the steps to deal with the enemy. If discipline is required, then it is given. There is no need ever to apologize when discipline is administered. The Bible says that our heavenly Father chastens those whom He loves. Chastening is a form of love. You are proving that you love a person enough to protect him from an enemy within or without.

There seems to be an idea that if you are strict with children and punish them, then you do not love them. The reverse is the truth. If you do not punish a child, you are cheating the child of his security and his own unsafe upbringing. The permissive cult is absolutely unscriptural. It is only of recent origin. Such people are the only creatures on God's earth who do not punish their young. All animals do, all "non-civilized" people do, all previous generations did. Much of this breakdown in society today is the harvest of the post-war doctrine of permissiveness. The generation gap has arisen largely because parents did not stay "in touch" with their children. If they had stayed "in touch" while they were growing up they would not be so out of touch now!

There are positive ways, also, in which the parents can cooperate with the great builder and keeper. Ephesians 6:10-13 says:

> *Finally, my brethren, be strong in the Lord, and in the power of his might.*
>
> *Put on the whole armour of God, that ye may be able to stand against the wiles of the devil.*
>
> *For we wrestle not against flesh and blood, but against principalities, against powers, against the rulers of the darkness of this world, against spiritual wickedness in high places.*
>
> *Wherefore take unto you the whole armour of God, that ye may be able to withstand in the evil day, and having done all, to stand.*

This passage warns us as to our enemies, who they really are—who is behind the drugs and the dirt that seeks to capture the minds of young and old. So insidious are the devious ways in which Satan is mounting his attacks on the hearts and the homes of all men everywhere today, that no man knows the full extent of his evil penetration.

The answer, in God's Word, is to be strong in the Lord, and in the power of His might. It then tells you how this can be done—by putting on the whole armour of God. The time to start this is as soon as a child can begin to understand, and the place is at the Family Altar, or the similar type of home worship —whatever it may be called.

Most little children enjoy or understand playing with

toy guns or other toy weapons of warfare. Some of these toys have a fearsome similarity to the real thing. In just the same way God's Word can be a simple handling of thoughts and ideas with which we can resist the enemy. The armor of God comes in all sizes! Don't wait until your children are grown before you try them on for size.

This in no way suggests we should emphasize Satan in our studies, but it does suggest we show them that being a Christian isn't the name of a game we play. We can certainly speak of the beautiful things of life and thank God for them, but we also need to remember that Satan starts to attack our children as soon as they are born. Don't give him a head start by spending the first five or six years talking only about birds and bees and flowers. Of course we will emphasize that God is love, but don't forget that the great characteristic of God is His holiness.

I have sensed a falling off in the use of the Family Altar in many Christian homes. As I speak with parents at family conferences I always find a curious interest in "how to" and "how not to" use this approach. Some have said they used to when the children were small, but then, as they got older "all things worked together for bad." There was resistance from the family, lack of time, and difficulty in coordinating time. Everyone thought it was an excellent idea—if only they could make it work.

Here are some suggestions that might help, or promote new thinking:

Start your "children's approach" as soon as number one can understand simple things and procedures. Make it part of the meal, build in a sense of incompleteness if you do not speak with Jesus. Don't make it too long at any time.

As children are older to junior level, gear the whole time to their level. Never make the family devotions a substitute for your own devotions. Make sure you do your own in your own time.

Learn and use some of the interesting techniques used in Sunday school for the age group concerned—games, competitions, quizzes, maybe a song or a chorus. If possible try to end while the children want more.

Make good use of prayer. Let the youngest pray first, in case all the topics are used up when his turn comes. Ask for prayer requests. Don't be afraid to pray for unusual topics such as birds with broken wings, or a sick puppy. One idea is to keep a record of when the prayer was made, then mark it off and date it when it is answered. This makes prayer itself not only worship and praise, but doing business with our heavenly Father. It is a good idea to appoint people to special duties, and don't forget to rotate the list. The prayer request secretary can be a really interesting office.

There are many good books today which offer simple Bible stories and studies, especially those in more simple language. Don't be afraid to start a discussion going. You will learn much about how your children think if you listen to their prayers and their comments. Don't be afraid to listen, and don't take all they say as exactly what they believe.

As your family becomes older it is an excellent plan to take turns in running the devotions. Have a routine pinned up on the board. Let the one in charge do exactly as he wishes—even as short as he wishes. Let him experiment, above all get each one to talk and discuss. Don't panic if subjects arise which scare you. If you do not have the immediate answer, say you will find out—and then seek God's help as you do so.

To achieve the best results start early, make it part of the meal, make it short and interesting, and be a good watchman in making sure your troops are disciplined. Don't surrender your position as head of the house to any rising opposition. Always remember that firmness promotes security, and that is what every young person needs more and more as the battle increases. If you do not give him security he will seek it elsewhere with some one, or some group.

In some cases it cannot be at meal times—because meals are staggered. In some cases it may seem impossible to hold the devotions daily. Don't give in too easily at this point. If something has to go, don't let it be Jesus!

Incidentally, don't be afraid to have a family hymn and song time. There is great fun in a singing family. You might even harmonize and be a family group. I met one such family recently in the Orient who had even made their own record. They enjoyed their singing so much that they shared it in churches and other groups. They were well worth listening to.

Above all, don't apologize for seeking to exalt Christ. Don't be ashamed of having such devotions. The Bible has a great deal to say about not being ashamed of Christ and His work. Likewise it says that God is not ashamed of such people.

In fact Psalm 127:5, speaking of the relationship between parents and their children says, "Happy is the man that has his quiver full of them: they shall not be ashamed, but they shall speak with the enemies in the gate." This phrase, "they shall not be ashamed," is a beautiful thought. It says that if there is this closeness of family relationship around the Person of Christ, neither will ever be ashamed of the other. The parents will not be ashamed of their children, and the children will not be ashamed of their parents.

This is exactly how you would want it to be; this is exactly how you can make it to be!

We were thinking before of putting on the whole armor of God. Verse 4 has some interesting thoughts in this connection: "As arrows are in the hand of a mighty man; so are children of the youth." The armor of God as listed in Ephesians 6 is all defensive. It describes the heavy protective armor of a Roman G.I. of those days—a breastplate, shield, helmet and sword. But when you speak of arrows, you are changing from the defensive to the offensive. No soldier will ever conquer if all he does is defend himself. The Christian soldiers who are "marching as to war" need more than protection, they need to be able to reach out and do battle for their Captain.

This is exactly what verse 4 is saying: "As arrows are in the hand of a mighty man; so are children of the youth." If the Lord builds your house and keeps your home, and if you are responsible laborers in His work then your children will be the arrows which God will use in His battle. When your children come to a genuine, living faith in Christ then they become arrows. The whole purpose of an arrow is to go where the soldier cannot reach. He aims his arrow at the target and away it goes reaching in and doing battle far beyond where he is standing. This is how the Lord can use your children as they witness and work for Him among friends, at school and college. You would never be able to get within range and communicate, but your children can. Don't forget that arrows can be all sizes.

Notice the teaching of verse 5: Happiness is a quiver full of arrows!—a family alive and alert for Jesus.

I have the opportunity to go to the mission fields of the world—India, Africa, South America, the Orient. These are the "target areas." It is here I see the arrows doing their work — brave, faithful missionaries battling on, in many cases, with heat, dirt, smells, disease and Satan himself. I watch them, and in many cases I am moved to tears as I see their unselfish loyalty to Christ. Then I remember where it all began. Somewhere, back home, their parents became laborers as they recognized the builder and the keeper of their home. In an unspectacular way they raised their family, but unknown to them God had His arrows in their family. In God's good time the arrows were aimed from the home and here they are on target.

I have spoken with many missionaries about their parents back home. Some of the stories are so homespun and unglamorous — just a farm in Kansas — a ranch in California — an office worker in Illinois — a teacher in New Jersey. Most of the parents are little "nobodies" in the eyes of the world. How wonderful to see it from the standpoint of heaven. Christian homes can be the arsenal of God, from which boys and girls and young men and women go forth to do battle for God.

This is why God builds and keeps the Christian home, so that He can use it in His plan to save a wicked, perishing world, to tell them of Jesus who died and rose again, to bring them to a knowledge of peace and power.

This is why you are a laborer for God—or are you?